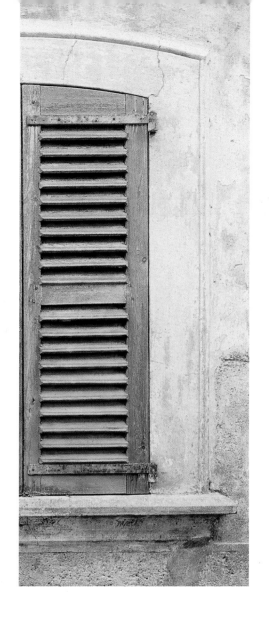

modern
rustic

modern
rustic

ideas for a natural lifestyle

ali hanan

photography by chris tubbs

published in association with

Livingetc

THE MODERN HOME & LIFESTYLE MAGAZINE

CASSELL&CO

contents

introduction

Modern rustic is not so much a style as a way of living. An ache for country has always resided in our bones; our urge to be associated with nature is instinctive, almost primal.

Even the most hard-core urbanite goes weak at the knees at the mention of a rural idyll, or just consider the set of emotions that follow as we escape on our fortnightly holiday. Sleek-minimalist loft apartments, chic suburban homes, and low-ceilinged offices are abandoned for back-to-basic beach huts, country cottages, French villas, and hideaways.

These refuges are our release valves, places where our senses and spirits are liberated and awakened. When we walk through the door of our rural haven, something forgotten is remembered. The interior is reassuringly familiar, like the embrace of a loved one.

Every age has had its Arcadian ideals. When Marie Antoinette and her entourage waltzed out to the *cottage* *orné*, it was merely a fashionable place to play pretend-peasant and live out faux-poverty fantasies.

In Regency England, when 'one' grew weary of city hubbub, country became the fashionable place to 'retire' (plus all the trappings, of course). Aristocracy aside, the modern love affair with rustic is more *real*. It's about reconnecting with the land, going back to basics, and rediscovering a lost heritage.

Moving to the country is not an option for most. Commitments chain urban dwellers to metropolitan and suburban environments. Yet if our feet are bound, why not rekindle our love affair with country living and introduce it into our everyday surroundings?

It makes sense: the more pressure-cooked our lives become, the more our homes need to resemble a bolt hole, a place where after a long day's work, we can regain a lost inner equilibrium; somewhere to simply go on vacation.

right: **Sweet sanctuary. The rural retreat provides sustenance for body and soul.**

modern versus rustic

'Architecture should speak of its time and place but yearn for timelessness'

architect Frank Gehry

When Englishman James Watt invented the steam engine in 1765, he created a behemoth. The machine was no giant, but its mechanics were responsible for igniting an entire revolution. The engine unleashed a new power – industrial mass-production – and the modern world was born. Cities suddenly grew exponentially, trains on freshly laid tracks stormed across the countryside, hotels proliferated, and administration buildings and worker barracks burgeoned. Life irrevocably changed.

Steamrollering into the following century, the industrial revolution continued unchecked. Most factories were replicating handmade designs with their new machinery, but one carpenter and entrepreneur, Michael Thonet, bucked the trend, paving the way for serial manufacturing. Harnessing the pressure of steam, he was able to bend beech staves into 'C' and 'S' shaped forms, and his lightweight, inexpensive 'Thonet chair', fashioned in 1859, became extremely popular. A staggering 50 million chairs were snapped up by 1930.

William Morris was horrified. At about the same time as the 'Thonet' inextricably changed furniture production, Morris, an Oxford-educated artist and poet, only saw 'the present development of civilization destroying the beauty of life'. Calling the industrial age 'a devilish capitalistic botch and an enemy of mankind', he

inspired a counter revolution, the Arts and Crafts movement, advocating a return to the rustic spirit of the Middle Ages when art, production, and nature were close allies. To him, industrialization had made a bitter impact on society: mass-produced goods were of poor quality, and badly paid sweatshops inflicted damage to workers. His firm Morris & Co championed naturally dyed cloth, hand-woven rugs, handmade tiles, and solid, simply produced furniture – a move towards a sophisticated rural style.

Across the Atlantic, the Shakers were the exemplars of a rustic approach. After fleeing persecution in England in the nineteenth century, the 'Quaking Shakers' established several communities in the United States. Believing that the beauty and perfection of heaven could be experienced by living simply and purely on earth, the communities continued to produce elegant handcrafted wooden furniture, disregarding all the technological advances and changing fashions of the 'outside' world.

In 1907 another revolution gripped the world of design: plastic. That year engineer Leo Baekeland developed Bakelite. Until then manufacturers had been entirely reliant on nature's materials to furnish and clothe interiors. But it wasn't until another decade later that plastic began infiltrating the ornate designs of the Art Deco era.

introduction   9

Into the 20s and 30s, the much-touted mantra of American architect Louis Sullivan 'form follows function' spurred design into a new realm. Modernism – mass-produced, functional, and streamlined design – made its debut. Functionalism became the new architectural buzzword, extolling that technical application rather than aesthetics should drive design.

At the helm were a string of architects – Frank Lloyd Wright, Le Corbusier, Marcel Breuer, Walter Gropius, Ludwig Mies van der Rohe, Adolf Loos, and later in the 50s, Charles and Ray Eames, and Arne Jacobsen. Their products were fashioned out of sleek new materials – glass, steel, moulded plywood and plastics – and their revolutionary geometric and angular shapes were a far cry from the countryside. Architect Hannes Mayer summed up the epoch with his quip that the house had become a 'machine for living'.

With the advent of Modernism, the cities became magnets for the bastions of the design intelligentsia. Country was left languishing at the starting block. City dwellers viewed the country as unfashionable, a resource for their building activities: country inhabitants spurned the city's new, vociferous consumerism.

The town-versus-country rift became a chasm. While 'city' was about utilitarian, tubular steel-framed furniture and modern technology, 'country' became viewed as stylized and staid, conjuring up clichéd images of gingham and chintz soft furnishings and, heaven forbid, unwieldy wooden beams groaning with dried lavender bunches.

rustic rebellion

As the 50s baby boom swung into action, suburbia, flushed with the first generation of post-war newly-weds, was clamouring for bright, inexpensive, household goods. A new wave of consumers cried out for innovative, timesaving technologies, craving anything 'high-tech'. And polypropylene, a malleable, light, inexpensive material, created by Giulio Natta and Karl Ziegler in 1952, answered the call. Polypropylene represented a shift in the public's attitude to design: man-made materials and objects were viewed as the hallmark of 'modern', and everybody coveted the products.

With the 50s taste for consumerism, planned obsolescence became spliced into production lines, encouraging a get-the-latest, keep-up-with-the-Jones' mentality. Polypropylene's first cousins – polyurethane, polyester and polystyrol – made an entrance as did colour TV (1951), and McDonald's (its first burger joint opened in Illinois). Urban streets were humming with optimism and 'progress'.

Then came the 60s revolutionaries. Rejecting the political, sexual, and social status quo, the 'beat' generation hit the road in search of a rawer, more primal experience. As political awareness grew, and the counterculture of American youth rebelled, they began shunning designers who they saw as being the instigators of mass-marketed, mass-fed, mass consumption. 'Flower power' ruled, as did 'back to basics', and the rebels embraced country with rock festivals springing up overnight on vast tracks of farmland. By the end of the decade, however, the

right: **Rediscover history. Objects from the past have virtues of strength and integrity.**

search seemed to lose its impetus: former upstarts were growing up, trickling back to the surbubs. Even, Ken Kesey, author and icon of the generation, opted out of the scene he'd been responsible for instigating, but instead of being sucked back into the city like his contemporaries, he hightailed it to his farm.

And then the oil crisis of 1973 crashed over the design world in a cataclysmic tidal wave. The attitude to plastics changed overnight: what was seen as the way forward suddenly became scorned. Consumers became more ecologically minded, seeking out alternative designs. Surges of rustic stamped their mark on the domestic scene with hip-to-it housewives making macramé planters and crocheting bedspreads. The interior palette became a mixture of mustards, earthy browns, and forest greens. 'Global warming' was a phrase uttered for the first time. An environmental awareness began to surface, as did the beginnings of the recycling movement and the first hankerings for a less synthetic, more natural world. Rustic was embraced – almost.

The 80s yuppie (young urban professional) wasn't interested. With big business booming in the early 80s, the trend was towards conspicuous consumption. The wealth was again concentrated in the city, where even the words 'the City' became a label for the central business district. The excess of cash ensured the death of Modernism as Postmodernism – eclecticism, pastiche, and ornamentation – stamped its mark on design. Showcasing, not domesticity, took centre stage, characterized by decoration (think matt black and gold leaf), and an 'emotional

response' to objects and 'designer' labels rather than designs. Country was simply a place to go for a long weekend. That is until Black Tuesday rocked the stock market off its pedestal in 1987.

With the curtain only just drawn on the last decade, what do we make of the 90s? The beginning of the decade wanted desperately to be different from the 80s. Living in a material world had proved to be spiritless and intrinsically unsatisfying. With 'the City' in tatters and the economic bubble burst, there was a collective soul-searching: what did we want?

For a while the answer was elusive. Interior magazines were striving to direct us, turning to the heady world of fashion for inspiration. Trends in interior design stormed off the catwalk into houses and apartments. But in our time-poor lives, who had the relentless appetite, or cash, let alone the time, to keep up with all fashion dictates?

Over the last few years home has become sweet again. Digging beneath the veneer of fashion, we have discovered of late that our homes are places for re-energizing, for nurturing body, mind, and soul. Subsequent environmental and health scares over the decade have concurrently demonstrated that we are living in a world of precious, precarious, ever-diminishing resources.

The end of the millennium has been characterized by retrospectives. Forced to reconsider our past, we are exhuming antiques and rejuvenating them, finding that they provide us with a sense of timelessness and continuity. We have come to realize that natural materials can be used in a modern way to create a fresh, beautiful

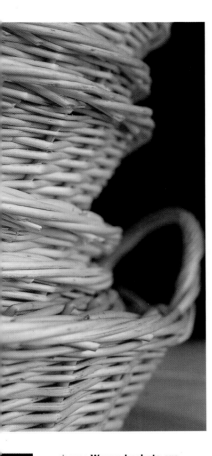

interior, and we are not afraid to choose them over man-made varieties.

Industrial revolution, petrochemical revolution – what next? The digital age is just beginning. But strangely instead of Stanley Kubrick's vision in *2001 A Space Odyssey*, we find the prospect of sophisticated technology tempered with a yearning, a *need* for the warmth of things with nature's touch. We appreciate Kahlil Gibran in *The Prophet*, who extols that our homes are not just the four walls around us but also include: 'the mansion of the sky, whose door is the morning mist and whose windows are the songs and the silences of night.' We have gone beyond surface design, realizing we are connected to a bigger picture, a part of the natural world around us. So what do we want next from our homes? We want modern rustic.

above: Woven baskets are not just 'country'. Alongside the new look wickerware, they can complement any modern interior.

left: Careworn and smooth, old things have exquisite textural qualities.

right: A converted barn pays tribute to the past life of the building. History and modern are woven together in an architecturally seamless way.

13

a modern interpretation

That authoritative tome, the dictionary, is perhaps the culprit for 'rustic' acquiring negative connotations. 'Rustic', it extols, is about 'having qualities prescribed to country life or people; simple, unsophisticated and crude…'

That's where it errs. Teamed with modernity, rustic can be incredibly sophisticated, but in a beautifully raw way that somehow has taken us decades to learn to appreciate. The look has infiltrated interior designers' consciousness almost inadvertently. Without even being aware of a rustic movement, fixtures and fittings have become simplified and elemental – yet still airily modern. Newly built loft conversions, for example, are harking back to their rural Scandinavian and Mediterranean roots, exposing wooden beams and swathing floors with terracotta tiles.

The materials are not new to us. Wood, tiles, plaster, stone, natural fabrics, and ironwork have been around for centuries. Those of us who are drawn to the modern rustic aesthetic don't want laminate worktops, synthetic carpets, and plastic accessories that have to be replaced every few years. We want the *real thing* and we want it to *last*. The cornerstones of rustic become more radiant with age and use: the patina of timber floors becomes handsome and silky to touch; stone weathers with dignity and grace; and iron mongery, even when rusty, keeps its look of functional sobriety. By surrounding ourselves with living, breathing, ecologically sound products our urban vistas regain a taste of the outside world.

Where 'out with the old, in with the new' was once the adage of fashion-followers, the philosophy driving the modern rustic aesthetic is almost converse: in with the old. However, instead of shunning all things modern, rustic plucks the best things from both worlds. It cherry-picks the cream of the past and splices into the mix the cutting-edge of present. The whole process doesn't happen overnight. Like the materials, it's organic.

And it doesn't cost much. Sometimes a couple of cushions, made from some leftover cotton swatches, or a wall painted in warm terracotta is all it takes. Rustic living is about materials not materialism; it's about action, not consumption.

above: Pitch rough weaves against raw wood to convey rustic's organic warmth.

sourcing, recycling, and restoring

Modern rustic style is about treasuring what we inherit, and appreciating that age has a beauty, and old things, made with quality materials, endure. Time is the best beauty treatment. Faded, peeling walls, old tiles, battered leather chairs, and worn, wooden floorboards all possess a certain charm that money cannot buy.

So where should you go to source the look? First, visit architectural salvage yards (places where builders and home renovators take everything they have stripped out of old houses, which can include anything from fireplaces to stained glass windows and pillar taps). These places are often situated outdoors, or in draughty barns, or warehouses.

below: Old pieces of furniture, and designs that pay homage to the past, ground this city townhouse.

To reap the best booty, get there early. The trick to getting the best out of the experience is to dress appropriately (old, warm clothes are recommended, as are gloves for rummaging through piles of items), take plenty of cash, a notebook with your home's specifications (room size, fittings sizes, etc.), and a tape measure.

Keep in mind that something that takes your fancy may cost just as much again to restore. Salvage yards sometimes offer on-site services, such as re-enamelling, polishing, shot blasting, delivering, and fitting, so negotiate extras into the price. Assess their condition first. Some things might only need a fresh coat of paint, or covering with new upholstery. And always haggle.

Other good picking grounds include flea markets, estate sales (the selling of a deceased person's property), and car boot sales. Again be prepared to barter. Take a measurement-filled notebook, and photos of your house, as these places often don't have a 'returns' policy. It's a case of 'see it, like it, buy it'.

Antique shops, junk stores, charity, and second-hand shops, internet auction sites, and markets are also bountiful hunting grounds. To find them, flick through the pages of your local paper. Specialist antique and interiors magazines, and other publications also yield good spoils: watch the 'For Sale' column religiously, and follow up whims.

Another element of modern rustic is to invest in organic products. To create the look, you need to go beyond the cosmetic, to investigate what the products you buy are made of. It's about furnishing the home with materials that nature intended us to

top left: Furniture is piled up high at a warehouse. Style often doesn't cost a lot, just the time to bring old pieces like these back to life.

bottom left: Old glass bottles can lead a double life as functional and decorative objects.

top right: **Flea markets and junk yards hold a key to the past.**

bottom right: **Covet antique fabrics woven from raw linen and wool.**

have, such as limewash paints, unbleached linens and cottons, and sustainable woods.

And it makes sense from a health point of view. A study in the United States of America demonstrated that some homes are over ten times more toxic than the outside world due to artificial paints and laminates offgasing, chemical residues from bleaches and detergents, and carbon monoxide emissions from leaking stove valves.

Support and commission young designers. At design fairs and through a rising number of interior shops, support innovators working with natural products. Become a patron of furniture makers, potters, metal workers, carvers, weavers, knitwear, and other craftspeople, who use traditional methods to produce contemporary designs.

Rustic style also embraces the *objet trouvé*. They merely cost the effort of picking them off the forest floor, beach, or riverbed, and taking them home in roomy pockets, buckets, or baskets. It sounds cliché but pine cones, stones from a beach walk, or dried autumn leaves, all bring in a little piece of nature. Place them strategically around the house so they catch your eye, evoke a memory, or make you smile.

The internet doesn't seem at first glance to be a rustic resource. It seems somehow ironic to be sitting in front of a computer screen purchasing from on-line auctions and surfing for supply outlets, but that's where technology makes our lives easier.

Utilize this vast sea of information to find out more about products, other like-minded people, and make an offer on goods. Use it wisely to source dealers, and then head outdoors.

rustic
elements

colour

When we let daydreams of escaping to our rural hideaway run riot, our mind's eye conjures up a palette of colours that walks arm-in-arm with the landscape. Just as in nature, rustic hues resonate with a quiet beauty. The colours we think of are never ersatz or gawdy. Instead, country tones are easy-going, sitting side-by-side like a couple of old friends.

the origins of colour

Right up until the last half-century, inspiration for colour originated from 'rustic' sources, dabbed directly from nature's paintbox. Ancient cultures used whatever was to hand. They utilized the yellow-red pigments of ochre and the bright reds of iron-rich hematite in decoration. The Egyptians crafted shades of green out of finely ground up malachite and made dusky yellows from orpiment. The Arabs powdered the semi-precious stone lapis lazuli to produce ultramarine, and abraded mercuric sulphide to create vermilion.

With the industrial boom after the Second World War, petrochemicals stole the limelight, leaving natural paints and dyes to gather dust. A coat of paint is the easiest way to transform an interior, and with modern demands for dry-faster, easy-to-apply washable finishes, synthetic-based dyes and paints are considered more convenient than traditional finishes.

Modern purists seeking to be in tune with the rustic ethos, however, can now select colour for interiors and furnishings from the new generation natural dyes and paints. Some possess man-made ingredients, but overall they are all biodegradable. Distemper, limewash, and milk paints, coloured with pigments derived from roots, bark, leaves, stems, and flowers such as camomile and saffron, as well as natural varnishes, waxes, and solvents, have been shoe-horned back onto shop floors and are readily available.

With completely organic paints, often – just as in nature – the colours age gracefully, and continue to look glorious even after years have passed.

the seasonal palette

Our perception of the rustic palette is like looking down a seasonal kaleidoscope. As Kahlil Gibran observes in *The Prophet*, inspirations ebb and flow with the seasons and light. 'Beauty shall rise at dawn from the east' … say the watchmen of the city. In the winter, say the snow-bound, 'She shall come with the spring, leaping from the hills'. In the summer the reapers say, 'We have seen her dancing with the autumn leaves, we saw a drift of snow in her hair'.

Choose the colours from each season that inspire you; then create a melange to suit.

right: Decorating made easy. Borrow colour inspirations directly from nature.

Summer, full of life, is strewn with cobalt blues, butter-coloured yellows, peaches, lilacs, burnt terracotta, verdant greens, and poppy reds.

With the fall, nature's autumnal canvas is layered in shades of mustard, apple green, rusty red, and rich earthy brown.

Cool neutrals such
as grey, taupe, and off-white
storm onto the winter scene,
and contrast with mahogany
tones and forest greens.

In spring a fanfare of clean colours –
lime greens, royal blues, and snowdrop
whites – mark a sense of freshness, a
time of rejuvenation. To our human eye,
each of these colours demarcates a
visual connection with 'rustic'.

Warm colours (ochres, peaches, mustards, and oranges) are perfect for social areas such as kitchens and dining rooms, while bedrooms and bathrooms, places to dream and relax, are suited to undemanding colours such as blues, lavender, and greens. Often choices depend on your experience of a colour: a blue bedroom may make one person relax but another shiver.

Think optical illusion. Remember the rules: warm colours advance, cool colours recede. In small, dark rooms, pale colours are expansive, making the most of the natural light. This doesn't work in a cramped, sunless room, however, as light paint may simply magnify the space's dinginess. Instead use vibrant shades such as mustard yellow or ruddy red.

neutrals

The most widely used neutral, white, has truly rural origins. It was once consigned to the humble bastions of rustic life: cowsheds, stables, and peasants' quarters. Throughout the day, however, it is as mutable as the seasons. As author Lewis Mumford once noted: 'At dawn, a white house is pale turquoise; at high noon it is clear yellow and lavender-blue; in ripe sunset it is orange and purple; in short, except on a grey day it is anything else but white.' Social critic, artist, and poet, William Morris, founder of the Arts and Crafts movement at the turn of the century, rejected busy frescoes and overbearing tapestries in favour of an 'honest whitewash … on which sun and shadow play so pleasantly'.

left: **Raw and elemental. This modern rustic living room effortlessly combines neutrals, from the exposed floorboards and brickwork to the coolness of the white walls and warm tones of the furnishings.**

right: **With its utilitarian crispness, white works well in any setting. Lavish it on walls, or juxtapose white details with rich, dark backgrounds.**

White matt has been the whitewash of the 90s minimalists. And its use has reached overkill. The words 'brilliant whites' are muttered in the same breath as 'contemporary furnishings', but these finishes are often too stark, too visually brittle. Soft chalky whites, created by traditional paints such as limewash and distemper, team better with a modern rustic look. Try other off-whites – creams, mushrooms, camels, and ivory – too. Not quite so 'edgy' as pure white, these neutral colours create backdrops that are soothing and calming, a visual balm. As legendary taste-shaper, Andrée Putman says, 'I love colours when they don't exist too much. Life always comes with its own colour: your friends, flowers, things. So you don't have to have so much of it in your own décor.'

Wood, plaster, stone, brick, and clay express the whole spectrum of neutral shades. In most cases, these natural materials should be left alone in the home to do what they do best: age. Instead of painting, give new or restored wood a facelift of linseed oil or sweet-scented beeswax (also an antistatic). Liquid beeswax embellishes the tones of cork, stone, and clay walls.

Create visual harmony. Use these neutrals as a calm backdrop and then inject colour through furniture and furnishings. For example, paint your walls taupe, then add accents of colour, such as apricot orange or olive green. On a practical level, using monochrome neutrals throughout a room makes it seem spacious. If a room is an odd shape, impartial hues painted on ceilings, walls, and skirting boards will cajole the eye into thinking the space seems flatter than it is.

paint

A fresh coat of paint over a wall will brighten up tired rooms, or rejuvenate old pieces of furniture (see pages 30–31 for details).

At one time, paint was literally a 'rustic' product. Paint pigments were obtained from sources such as the earth (ochre), plants (turmeric, rose madder), and mineral deposits (viridian, cadmium yellow). Binders were also based on 'found' materials such as chalk, lime, linseed oil, egg, and milk solids; glaze binders (transparent paints) even included household staples such as flat, dark ale and vinegar.

Superseded by synthetic, acrylic, and latex applications, these traditional paint ingredients were all but abandoned. Over time, however, they have proved to be just like plastics: they live hard then die young. As they age, the colours lack depth and character.

When coated on a wall, synthetic paints create a plastic-like skin, which creates an impermeable barrier with the underlying surface. Organic and biodegradable paints have the advantage of allowing a surface to breathe. Although slow to dry, the skin of the paint seeps into the underlayer, creating a permeable air exchange surface that allows natural ventilation to occur. Some natural pigments fade in the sunlight, creating a worn patchy look, but generally their patinas, like good wines, mellow with age.

Two ideal 'rustic' paints are limewash and distemper. Limewash, used originally by peasants and farmers, has anti-bacterial properties, and was once lavished on kitchens, pantries, cellars, and stables. It dries to a soft, velvety 'bloom', evocative of Spanish and Italian houses. Use limewash on rendered walls, old and new plaster, brickwork, skimmed walls, cement, concrete bricks, and previously painted surfaces.

Distemper, a popular wall paint throughout the centuries, is a water-based paint made from chalk, and has a matt, powdery finish. For the best results, apply as a wash over a base of untinted distemper.

Part of traditional paint's charm offensive is its sense of informality and ease. Besides the 'broken' colour effects of distemper, there are a number of other techniques that create a mottled or uneven finish. Instead of using the mechanical (and clichéd) rag n' roll effect, rub paint into the wall with a cloth. Another way is to apply successive layers of diluted water-based paint with thick brush strokes. For a finish that recalls plaster or sandstone, add crushed olive pips to the paint mix for a look sensual to both the eye and fingertips.

Live with a colour before you commit to it. Before buying, try out 'test blocks', painting various one-metre squares in different areas of the room. Throughout the day observe the daylight play on the paint, note the kind of mood evoked, and your innate response to it – and then make your decision.

right: A coat of paint provides an instant lift. In this room a vibrant shade of blue has been applied with thick brush strokes to create a rough, beautiful finish.

ocean blue

corn-flower

morning sky

forest green

sage green

cool mint

dark earth

black berry

winter sky

russet red

provence ochre

spicy paprika

painted chair

This is an excellent way of giving inexpensive furniture a rustic makeover. This process can be applied to a chair, table, or cupboard.

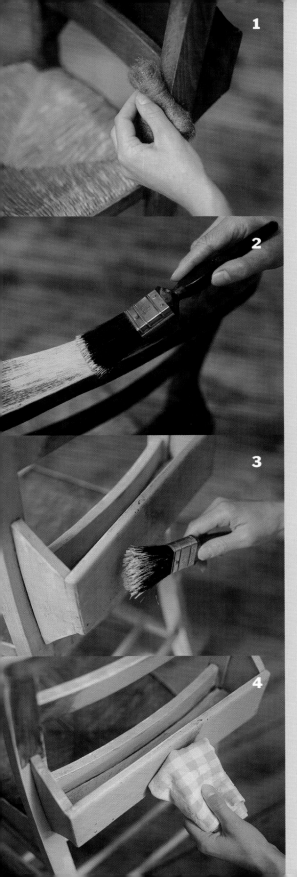

1 Prepare the chair by removing any old wax and varnish with a rag or wire wool and methylated spirits, and allow to dry.

2 Using a dry brush, apply a thin layer of off-white emulsion paint as an undercoat, allowing the character and age (i.e. the grain and any knocks and blemishes) of the chair to show through. Leave to dry for approximately five hours, then apply an even coat of acrylic crackle glaze and allow this to dry overnight.

3 Roughly apply a thick coat of pale green emulsion paint in as few strokes as possible. As the emulsion begins to dry cracks will start to appear. These can be exaggerated by speeding up the drying process with a hairdryer. Leave to dry for another five hours.

4 Mix a solution of half-and-half eggshell varnish and white spirits and mix this with a little raw umber artist's oil paint. Paint this solution onto the chair a section at a time; leave to dry for a few minutes, then wipe away any excess with a rag, leaving behind a brown 'dirty' residue in the recesses. This will accentuate the character of the wood and give a more authentic rustic look. (If you go wrong you can wipe the solution away with white spirits before it dries and start again.) Leave to dry overnight. Protect and finish the chair with a coat of eggshell varnish mixed with a small amount of white artist's oil paint to give it a dusty, aged appearance.

YOU WILL NEED:
* Old wooden chair or similar piece of furniture
* Wire wool
* Methylated spirits
* Selection of paintbrushes and old rags
* Off-white emulsion (water-based) paint
* Acrylic crackle glaze (available in good DIY and paint stores)
* Pale green emulsion paint or colour of your choice
* Oil-based eggshell varnish
* White spirits
* Raw umber artist's oil paint (available from art stores and craft shops)
* White artist's oil paint

textures + materials

Felled, quarried, hewn, or harvested materials, such as wood, plaster, brick and stone, literally have their roots in nature. Wood, left in its primal state, exposed brick, weathered timber boards, and handmade tiles directly express country qualities. They are naked, unadorned, simple, and honest.

rustic building blocks

Architecture in the past worked with local materials. In medieval Europe, peasants' dwellings were crafted by spreading a mixture of damp earth and straw over wattle panels, which, once dried by the sunlight, were smeared with a thick coating of limewash. Timber and thatch were the favourite building blocks of the Maoris of New Zealand; the Scandinavians, whose pinewood look is still in vogue, harnessed their forests, lashing together tree trunks to create massive log cabins. In North America, the plentiful wood supply meant that settlers' homes were also founded on timber: the homes of New England were – and still are – typically timber-framed, clad with clapboard and topped off with cedar shingles on the roof. Mexican and African cultures still utilize adobe and earth; and in certain regions of Britain, stone houses are still built according to local quarry sources. Limestone graces the dwellings of the Cotswolds; dark, moody slate dominates Welsh interiors; granite gives Cornish interiors their regional flavour.

History counts. Just as human faces become etched with lines portraying experience and emotion, so the interiors of a house reveal a story: before embarking on any decorating, cherish your home's inherited characteristics. Cracked plaster walls, weathered floorboards and flagstones worn smooth with countless footfalls are all 'character lines', giving a house an idiosyncratic past. A home's bones are often its most beautiful attributes, so where you can, delve under surfaces and discover hidden gems beneath. Where possible, reclaim original flooring, and strip back wall coverings to expose stone and reveal brickwork.

To attain the rustic feel, you don't have to overhaul a whole room: the trick is to convey variety, to invite nature onto walls and floors. Combine visual with tactile elements to add depth and contrast, and enhance a richness of mood. Vinyl floor coverings, synthetic carpets and plastic wall coverings don't last the distance. Why buy fake wood cladding which will have to be replaced every five years when the real thing lasts a lifetime? Man-made substitutes don't breathe and their colours just don't mingle easily with the rustic look. Cool in the summer, insulating in the winter, natural materials resonate with the weather. Their textures, colours and aromas are peerless.

top: The wooden bones making up the roof of an English barn.

above: A tiled roof in Provence.

left: Smooth, sculptural walls, fashioned from adobe.

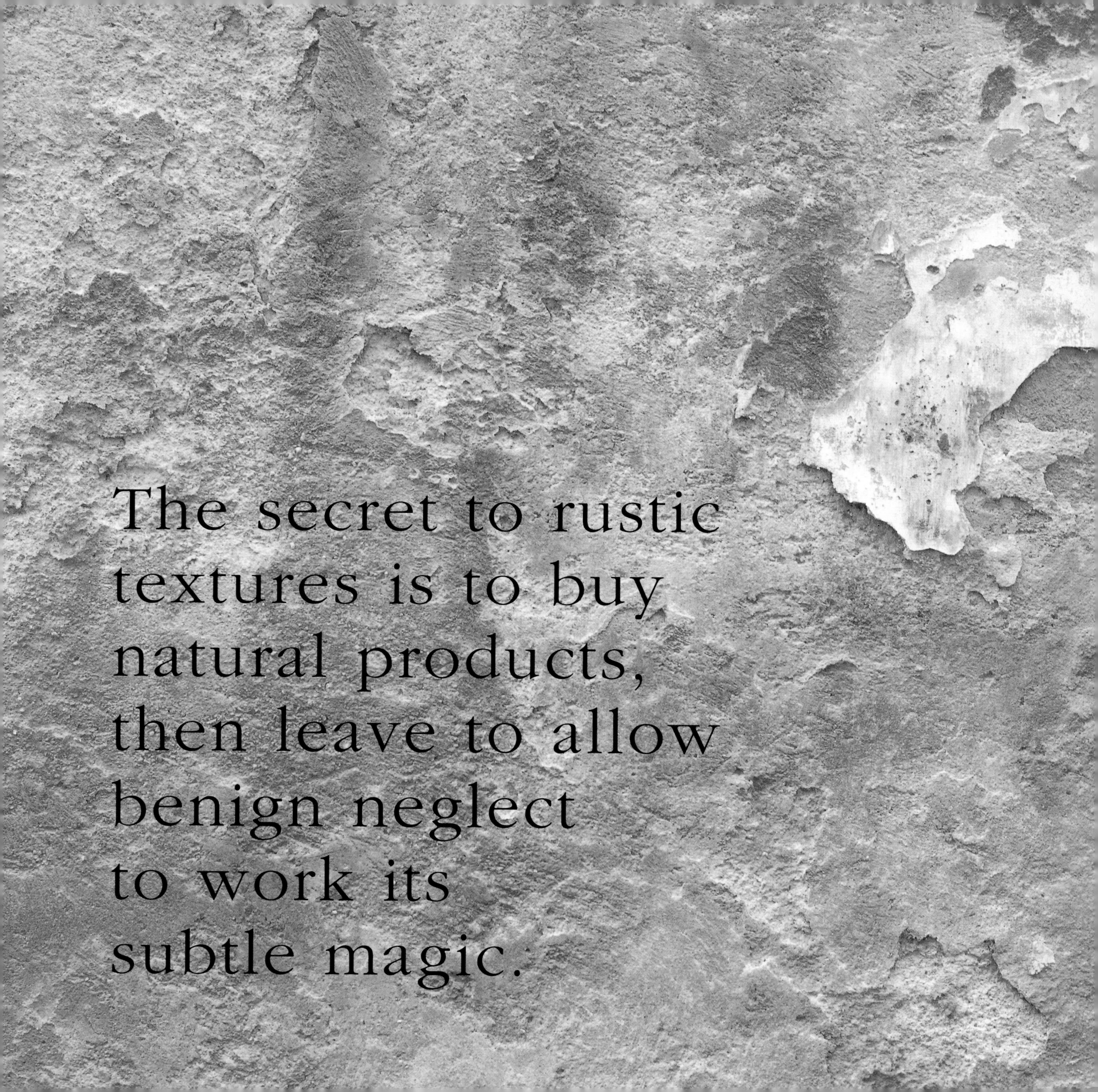

The secret to rustic
textures is to buy
natural products,
then leave to allow
benign neglect
to work its
subtle magic.

nature's materials

Floors and walls are the backdrops to which we play out our lives. Floors – one of a home's visual attractions – are essential to get right. When selecting floors, tailor materials to suitable areas: pure wool carpets are soft underfoot and kind to young knees but are prone to staining, so use them in living rooms and bedrooms. For alternative hard-wearing floor coverings, consider matting and rugs woven from other natural fibres such as coir, jute, and sissal. Brick, wood, and tiles withstand the daily rigours of household traffic and so labour best in entrance halls, kitchens, bathrooms, and areas of indoor-outdoor transition.

Walls are the canvases for an entourage of fittings and pictures. To avoid visual noise, keep them simple. For interest, employ a tactile surface such as rough wood-cladding or raw plaster, and leave nude. Remember the motto 'less is more': textural patterns in natural materials tend to take on a captivating charm of their own.

Wood has always been the coveted material of the country. Forests once blanketed the land and their products – branches, leaves, resin, and trunks – were harnessed for everything from fabrics to fencing. Timber allows natural ventilation – it breathes, purifying the air, and emits a beautiful, soothing scent. Before you buy new woods, first scout out salvage and reclamation yards for recycled timber – old woods are often thicker, better-seasoned, and richer in patina.

left: Functional and evocative. Large Welsh slate tiles on the floor and brick walls combine to create visual harmony. In the winter, underfloor heating warms the stones providing a sensual surface for the soles of the feet.

right: Flooring *au naturel*. Tiles in this Provençal retreat reflect the ochre-red colour of the earth typical of the area.

Rustic style is about looking after the countryside's resources. Ensure you only buy sustainable woods: for example, in the United States 'old growth' is the term applied to trees from ancient forests including Douglas fir, redwood, and red cedar, but only 5 per cent of these evaporating forests are left intact.

Although loved for their practical construction-favoured qualities (redwood resists rot; cedar is water-repellent as a roof shingle; fir is incredibly strong), conservationists in the United States now advocate only using 'second growth' forests, such as oak, elm, pine, spruce, and walnut, which have their own inherent virtues. Unless salvaged, never buy mahogany, teak, rosewood, liana, and ebony. These are also on the endangered list.

Once laid or exposed, sand boards to a smooth finish and then wax or varnish, stain or paint. For a soft-white Scandi-style feel, apply a gentle wash of organic diluted emulsion. Apply stains made from plant extracts and then treat with shellac, a natural varnish, or lazur, a translucent wood protector made from plant oils and herb extracts. Wax with beeswax for an aromatic, anti-static finish.

Wood has other cousins – cork and linoleum. Cork is produced by stripping the bark of the cork oak *Quercus suber* (a sustainable resource), and also has sumptuous tones. Linoleum is made from a number of nature's ingredients – powdered cork, linseed oil, wood flour, chalk, and wood resins – all pressed onto a hessian backing. These ingredients give it strength and durability – lino also has the advantage of

left: A dying art. One of the last remaining workshops of handmade tiles in southern France. The direct connection between maker and nature reflects in the beauty of the craftsmanship.

possessing antiseptic properties (it was once commonly used in hospitals), and is anti-static.

The price tag of stone can be off-putting, but, unlike anything else, it endures and is worth the investment. Use on walls as a textural backdrop, or on floors for a hassle-free long-life surface. Some varieties are more porous than others so check with the dealer whether yours will need sealing to prevent staining. To upkeep its looks, wax stone with liquid beeswax.

Tiles and bricks were once made with the flux of the seasons. In medieval times, as Elizabeth Hilliard documents in *The Tile Book*: 'Clay was dug out of the ground in the autumn, turned in the winter, then worked into tiles in the spring. In the meantime, the tile-making workshops

and kilns were being prepared. Tile blanks were cut, then dried outdoors or in a shed kept warm with a fire before being decorated, trimmed, glazed and fired.'

Today, handmade bricks and tiles are more expensive than machine-made products, but the human spirit often finds the perfection of mass-produced pieces artificial and lifeless. To source, head to specialist shops or architectural salvage yards. Tiles are available in an enormous variety of sizes, glazed or unglazed, plain or decorative. Use in splashback areas, on floors, or worktops for kitchen areas. The earthy hues of brick bring ocular warmth to floors and walls: for visual rhythm and a textural look on floors, lay bricks in patterns such as herringbone or basket weave.

fabulous fabrics

When rustic is at its most pure, the look can be quite hard, even stark. Introducing fabrics is a way of injecting a soft modernity and tempering hard edges with a twist of femininity.

In our rustic past, all clothing, furnishings, and bedding were derived from organic sources. Some of the earliest examples of European textiles date from the Neolithic period (4000–2000 BC), discovered on the shores of the Swiss lakes, where elm and oak fibres were woven into cloth for garments as well as fishing nets and baskets. Nature's products for weaving, spinning, knitting, tapestry, lace-making, embroidery, and felt-making stemmed from animals (sheep, goats, the silkworm, cows, rabbits), and plants (cotton, linen, flax, hemp, rush, papyrus reeds). Yarns were dyed using by-products from crushed leaves, crushed insects, minerals, and powdered plants: saffron and tumeric created yellow, the madder root created reds, indigo and the plant woad created blues and purples.

No matter how sophisticated man-made fibres have become, their natural relatives seem somehow superior. The simple fact is that light, air, and aroma pass though them freely. Think of sweating in a polyester shirt compared to the relief of breathable cotton on a humid day.

Natural dyes are also infinitely preferable to their synthetic cousins. If not fastened properly, they fade, but do so with dignity, still blending in with the rustic aesthetic. If natural dyes are unavailable, at least choose colours from nature's palette as a happy compromise.

top left: A cashmere (fine goat's wool) throw makes a good bed partner to curl up with.

middle left: A modern take on check patterns in cotton, suitable for soft furnishings.

bottom left: A hundred-year-old quilt, fashioned from a cast-off full-length skirt.

right: Natural fabrics, from the bed spread down to the linen dressing gown, instil a sense of freshness, lightness, and ease.

wools, linens, cottons, silks

In the natural fabric intelligence stakes, wool wins hands down, which is why nomads of Africa and Asia have used it as a building material for tents for centuries. Still today, the Inner Mongolian nomads' *yurta* (tents) are crafted from felt, created by matting woollen fibres together. Resilient, incredibly strong, and flame resistant – extraordinarily – a wool fibre can also be bent up to 30,000 times without being damaged. Although wool absorbs as much as 30 per cent of its weight in moisture, damp wool is a natural insulator – its outer surface releases vapour through evaporation. Pure carpets, made from

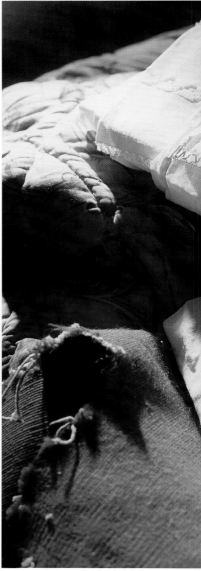

top left: **Linen feels *right*. Snuggle up with linen bed sheets, or use it for napkins and tea towels.**

bottom left: **For a feminine twist, add a little handmade lace.**

coarser wool from sheep breeds such as the Romney, are resilient and hard-wearing, while Australia, which produces one-third of the world's wool, is home to the Merino, which yields a soft, high-lustre yarn, spun into the finest blankets and sweaters.

Linen is moisture resistant (and even stronger when wet), cool, and durable. The fibres from the flax *linum usitatissimum* have been lauded since earliest recorded history: remnants of the fabric were unearthed in Egyptian tombs. In Europe, from the seventeenth to the nineteenth centuries, linen was a status symbol: a bride's linen trousseau was worth its weight in gold. After the First World War, with the rise of easy-care cotton, linen lost its pole position. Stashes of the once coveted heirlooms are now surfacing at flea markets and specialist shops, which are the best places to go for real time-softened linens and handmade laces.

Other natural fabrics include soft cottons from the seed pods of the annual *Gossypium*, and luxuriously light silk from the silkworm (silk strands are even finer than the human hair). As a contrast, the rough weaves and tawny-brown to olive-green shades of horsehair, hemp, and hessian also add a rugged feel to a rustic-style interior for floor coverings and drapes.

soft furnishings

Use fabrics to introduce life and colour in rhythm with the rustic ethos. Opt for those coloured with natural dyes such as madder root or camomile, or play peasant and cut up old shirts and sew them into patchwork covers. Use faded floral cottons,

cambric, and lawn for a lightweight throw; tweeds, woollens, worn-out denims, and animal skins (real or fake) for a cosy winter blanket.

Dress your rooms or reinvent them according to the season. Change cushion covers, slip covers, bed linen, floor coverings, and tablecloths in tune with the yearly cycle. Fabrics are sensual essentials in the boudoir. The winter bedroom should be like a fur-lined nest – hibernate with delicate linens and thick feather-filled duvets – while in summer, change to fine silk sheets and soft mohair blankets.

Textured cushions are as easy to make as our project on pages 44–45. Loose fitting covers for chairs are also simple. First make a plan on dressmaker's layout paper for the dimensions of each piece. Try a dummy run and pin, fit the paper sections in place on the chair, then, once you're happy, cut out each piece of fabric, test out on chair, then pin, fit, and sew the cover together. To save having to make another in a hurry, use robust, hard-wearing fabrics such as calico and heavy cotton.

Sometimes covering just the seat is another quick facelift remedy. Cut two pieces of fabric large enough to cover the seat area, allowing a sufficient seam allowance. Sew with right sides together, leaving one side open; turn right side out, and press. Cut a piece of wadding just slightly smaller than the cushion cover and insert, before sewing up. Sew a length of cotton tape to each corner to tie the cushion to the chair uprights. Neaten the cushion if you like, by sewing a length of tape around the outside edge of the cushion.

patchwork cushion

Choose from a variety of fabric pieces mixing colours, patterns, and textures for this project. Fabrics that work well together include knobbly woollen tweeds, flannels, and plaids. Pitch checks against stripes, or herringbone against plain.

1 From a selection of fabrics, cut four 30cm/12in square patches (or alternatively cut out four pieces of fabric measuring 17.5 x 55cm/7 x 22in to make a rectangular pattern).

2 Place two patches right sides together, and pin along one edge. Machine stitch and press the seam open. Repeat with the remaining two patches. Pin the two pieces right sides together along one long side, then machine stitch and press the seam open to make a square panel for the front of the cushion. Place one rectangle of corduroy right side down with the longest sides at the top and bottom, and fold back an overlap of 10cm/4in. Pin and hem stitch. With your sewing machine, make four buttonholes 2.5cm/1in in from the fold equidistant apart.

3 Place the second rectangle of corduroy face down in the same way and turn back an overlap of 5cm/2in. Pin and hem stitch. Turn the fabric over and stitch the wooden buttons in place 2.5cm/1in in from the fold, taking care that the distance between the centre of each is equal to the distance between the buttonholes. With right sides together, pin the top and bottom edges of the cushion back to the front panel, and machine stitch allowing 2.5cm/1in for a seam allowance. Press the seams open.

4 Carefully pin and machine stitch the sides with a 2.5cm/1in seam allowance, making sure that the buttonholes will overlap the buttons correctly when turned right side out. Turn the cover right side out and press before inserting the cushion.

YOU WILL NEED:
For a 50cm/½yd square cushion

* Fabric scraps measuring at least 30cm/12in square
* Two pieces of chunky corduroy measuring 37.5 x 55cm/15 x 22in
* Four wooden buttons
* Sewing machine
* Sewing kit
* Iron

furnishings + storage

Think of the moment

when, after fleeing to our rustic hideaway, we unpack, pour ourselves a warming drink, and then flop into the embrace of an old armchair. Moulded by countless bodies – unlike its sleek modern counterparts – the rustic chair is easy and intimate. On closer inspection, we can see the hallmarks of this favourite piece of furniture: leather battered by countless 'seats' and worn silky smooth to the touch; fabric thinning, then patched. All these details are telltale signs of durability and comfort.

rustic renaissance

We expect high standards from our furnishings. As Julie Iovine advises in *Chic Simple: Home:* 'In the ergonomics of everyday life, the chair plays a central role. It props you up for breakfast; braces you at a desk; cradles you in comfort at the end of a long day. With each new function, the chair's shape undergoes a dramatic shift in personality.' The kitchen table is an equally important piece of furniture. Particularly with the death of the formal dining room, and the rise of the all-in-one kitchen-cum-living room, the table is a chameleon, playing the role of breakfast table, study space, and dinner party host.

Once-upon-a-rustic-setting, furniture was basic. A historical overview shows us that when nature's booty entirely sustained us, all we needed were tree trunks and rocks to rest our haunches

on, and piles of hay, ferns, or hide to sleep on.

Until the Industrial Revolution, furniture was entirely handmade out of wood, stone, and leather, and covered with delicate hand-stitched tapestries. Then mass manufacturing changed the face of furniture production with the 'Thonet' chair, the first example of 'bent wood furniture'.

Furniture changed again with the invention of plastic in 1907. It wasn't until the rise of petro-chemical manufacturing after the Second World War that plastic furnishings became a coveted household staple, and continue to be so today.

Modern rustic style, however, is about solid, built-to-last furniture pieces made from the earth's wares. The case for banning plastic furnishings from a country-cum-urban interior is a strong one. Where plastics become scratched, scarred, and defaced with use, wooden chairs gain softness and personality. Once broken, plastic furniture is difficult to fix – we toss it aside (hardly environmentally friendly), whereas wooden furnishings can be easily repaired, repainted, or reupholstered.

So when selecting furniture, choose wisely. Hark back to our rural roots and choose furniture made from wood, and alternatives such as bamboo, cane and wicker, or stone, and metal, and covered in natural fibres. You'll find it easier to live with, durable and lasting – all virtues essential in modern homes.

left: An old leather Paris club chair reclines in a casual setting waiting for someone to cradle.

foraging for furniture

To get the look, first consider the setting.
Juxtapose items against the kind of interior you
have. Think of the typical furnishings of a
country cottage: mismatched and uncoordinated,
yet somehow close colleagues. How does the look
work? By introducing a variety of furniture pieces
which simply have lovely shapes, organic flowing
lines, contrasts of hard (wood frames) and soft
(upholstery), light and dark, and rough and
smooth, furnishings in a room chosen with a
consistent look in mind, create their own harmony.
Don't force it, just pick pieces that you love: by
following your own sense of taste you'll
unconsciously select a consistent visual mish-mash.
And remember that it doesn't have to cost much.
Heed the words of visionary interiors guru Andrée
Putman: 'Unless you have a feeling for the secret
knowledge that modest things can be more

above: **Simple wooden seats make excellent dining companions.**

left: **A coffee table surface is decorated with roofing studs, nails, and tacks in a range of copper, steel, and galvanized wire.**

right: Tree trunks, old wooden gates, and found objects from skips, beaches, and junk yards are all being fashioned into rustic furniture by today's inventive designers.

overleaf left: A slatted wooden chair is an extremely versatile item of furniture. Use indoors or out, or even as a pedestal for flowers.

overleaf right: Choose a generously large sofa to stretch out on. The chair toward the bottom left-hand corner is awaiting a revamp. Selected for its shape, simply reupholstering it will give the chair a new lease of life.

beautiful than anything expensive, you will never have style.'

Hark back to the past. Cherished antiques sit just as comfortably in a home built yesterday, as they do in one built a hundred years ago. When sourcing antiques, however, have patience. Discovering the *right* antique takes time. Enjoy the thrill of the chase. Hire a van and go on a hunt, scouring car boot sales, flea markets, second-hand stores, charity auctions, and estate sales, scouting out things with *soul*.

Often old pieces can be easily updated. A chair with a ripped seat cover is easily repaired; perhaps even 'modernize' an old piece by giving it a makeover with some fabric in a simple check or floral pattern.

If old or antique furniture is not to your taste, try the sculptural lines of modern furniture crafted from wood, cane, wicker, and metal. To source, first try seeking out handcrafted goods. Support the synergy of maker and material by championing the work of young furniture designers who explore the use of natural products in a contemporary way. Or look around interior and garden stores for natural products with a modern bent. Often outdoor furnishings, such as wicker tables and wooden slatted chairs, work equally well indoors.

If nothing takes your fancy, go straight to nature. Reclaim a few old trunks from a wood yard, then sand and varnish (see pages 58–59 for details) for some elegant rudimentary seating. For a low-level table, find an old door, sand it down, and take it to a carpenter or metal worker to attach some legs.

'Style is to see beauty in modest things.'

Andrée Putman

left: The strong sculptural shapes of these wicker chairs complement the wood and stone interior in this converted barn.

right: A popular and practical choice in modern homes is the farmhouse table.

below: A plain chest is covered with handmade papers in soft wood-toned colours, and fitted with handles made from strong weathered oak twigs.

particular pieces

One of the most coveted staples of rustic is the farmhouse table – even in chic modern interiors. Generously wide, sturdy, and long, it has a forthright, robust character with no formal airs or pretentions. The larger it is, the more of an anchor it becomes, but if space constraints dictate otherwise, opt for a drop-leaf table to economize.

Occasional tables such as side tables, stacking tables, and bedside tables provide convenient surfaces for tailored activities, or to act as areas of display.

With chairs, the ultimate deciding factors should be function and ease. As architect Ludwig Mies van der Rohe famously stated: 'A chair is a very difficult object to design. A skyscaper is almost easier, which is why Chippendale is so famous.' The only way to be sure of a chair's character is to take it for a test drive. What isn't comfortable after five minutes won't improve after fifty. However, bear in mind that soft furnishings, squabs, and cushions can allay hard edges.

Restore what you've inherited by using crackled paint effects, or strip away the previous coats of paint, and varnish, oil, or wax the wood. Reupholstering chairs and sofas also gives them a new lease of life: create visual dichotomy by mixing modern materials with classic shapes. As long as the basic structure of the piece is sound, it is worth re-covering.

Choose roomy, well-proportioned sofas, day beds, or chaise longues for the living room. Snap up weathered old leather sofas and armchairs if you can find them at markets – these old-timers last forever. Soften hard chairs or benches by sewing up old scraps of fabric and making them into feather-filled cushions, or mix in textural interest and protective cover with old shawls, mohair blankets, and fur throws. In the dining room rustic-style garden furniture, bent wood chairs, and slatted metal framed wooden chairs all bring a touch of country elegance.

furnishings + storage   53

storage

As rustic is about simplicity and space, so is good storage. And when it comes to creating space, a little organization goes a long way. With modern urban spaces becoming increasingly smaller, smart storage is key. Keep to the modern rustic ethos and don't clutter spaces with spanking new plastic containers and precarious cardboard boxes, or spoil the look with ultra-modern cupboards. Instead, be inspired by history and nature.

Before built-in cupboards were first designed in the early nineteenth century, storage was about flexibility – and it still should be. In the Middle Ages, households stashed their possessions in all-purpose chests, which lead a double life as tables and beds. Storage items housed everything, particularly the goods of tradesmen and retailers, who, in order to advertise their products, paid meticulous attention to packaging their wares. In the market place, apples were placed in wooden stacking trays, designed to be reused over and over again; on the farm, eggs, vegetables, and fruits were collected in commodious wicker baskets.

left: **Hide things away in decorative pots and jars, but strike a balance, leaving some things, such as the almost sculptural magnetic knife rack, on display.**

right: **A place for everything, and everything in its place. A benevolently sized nineteenth-century cupboard unit can still be put to good use.**

Rescue and reinvent the past. Stow your possessions in wooden hatboxes, wickerwork baskets, leather trunks, metal pails, and oval Shaker boxes constructed with elegant swallowtail joins. Salvage old wardrobes and cupboards and rejuvenate them with a new coat of paint. If you have to buy totally new cupboards, add a rustic twist with reclaimed doorknobs, pull handles, or unusual brass or iron hinges. If your cupboards are open fronted, either show off your treasures behind glass, or hide them, attaching an old piece of lace or hessian gathered on a pole or length of wire.

top left: **The Shakers are renowned for their penchant for functionality. Their peg rails have proved an enduring legacy, and are handy in today's kitchen for avoiding bench-top clutter in small spaces.**

top middle: **A sturdy wire basket doubles as a magazines tidy.**

top right: **Stash a wicker hamper under the bed to store seasonal clothes. Like many natural materials, wicker breathes, and so keeps garments aired and fresh.**

bottom left: **Old hatboxes provide great storage, and can masquerade as a tabletop.**

bottom middle: **Blood relations of the classic club chair, antique leather cases are equally timeless. Use for storing papers and documents in the home office.**

bottom right: **A farmhouse pail is re-employed for stowing logs by the fire.**

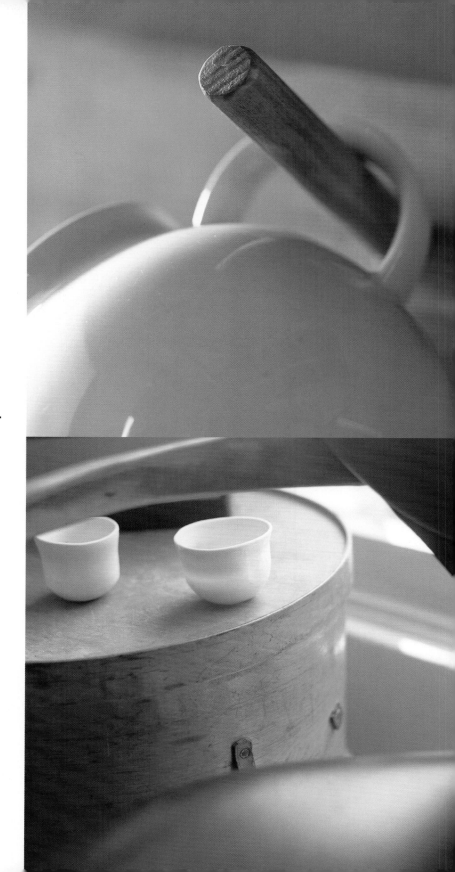

rugged stool

This is a simple, sculptural piece of casual seating that allows the natural beauty of the wood to shine through.

1 Lever the bark off the timber using a hammer and chisel as gently as possible so as not to dent the surface beneath.

2 Sand the surface of the timber until it is smooth to the touch with the electric sander using firm circular motions. Go carefully and be patient.

3 Wipe away any dust with a damp cloth, then apply an even coat of clear satin wood varnish and leave to dry.

4 The varnish brings out the grain of the wood, which will feel rough to the touch again. Sand back by hand using very fine sandpaper. Apply another coat of varnish and leave to dry. You may need to repeat this process several times to acquire a smooth protective finish.

YOU WILL NEED:
* **Large piece of raw timber measuring approximately 40–45cm/16–18in in height, with a diameter of 35cm/14in (you can obtain this from salvage and timber yards)**
* **Cold chisel**
* **Hammer**
* **Electric sander (you can sand by hand but this will take considerably longer)**
* **Damp cloth**
* **Clear satin finish wood varnish**
* **Paintbrush**
* **Piece of fine grade sandpaper**

light + shadow

When we lived close to the rhythms of nature, our lives revolved around the cycle of the sun (rising at first light, retiring soon after dark). Nowadays office-bound jobs and artificial light have divorced us from this natural cycle. Statistics have revealed that today most of us spend 90 per cent of our time indoors, under the relentless scowl of artificial lights in workplaces and homes.

All of us – even indoor inhabitants – still unwittingly respond to seasonal light variations. In the summer we innately 'make hay while the sun shines', while in winter, when the sun is one-tenth its intensity, we tend to slow down physically and spiritually.

At its worst, light deprivation can offset Seasonal Affective Disorder (SAD), where sufferers experience increased somnolence, fatigue, emotional flatness, and lethargy. Travel operators, recognizing the glaring absence of outdoor light in most workers' lives, accordingly create luring escapes where urbanites can 'run to the sun': sunshine is the draw card.

Because we are affected by natural light, it makes sense to organize the rooms in our homes to maximize its potential. Social hubs such as kitchens and living rooms are best bright and sun-filled, while bedrooms only need ambient light – they must be dark enough to allow the sleeper to dream.

If light is important, so is its antithesis: shadow. We need dark places to think. Shadow in a room creates depth, and emphasizes sculptural shapes, making our perception of a space more meaningful. When positioning windows and lights, think about casting shadows on walls.

a window on the world

The natural light from windows gives our interiors life. Yet they don't just provide us with a sense of day and night: they are our umbilical cord to the outside world. In the past, country cottage windows were small and few, due to concerns about heat loss, the expense of glass, and the fact that so much time was actually spent outdoors. That's where modern times – and reasonably priced glass panes – has changed our attitude toward rustic. Today the best windows are the biggest. The law even requires that all 'habitable' rooms must have one, acknowledging that without views to the exterior world we are somehow deprived. Air, light, and a view of the outside world are intrinsic to our wellbeing.

Make windows where you can by punching out skylights (you often don't need planning permission if you're not changing the shape of the roof, but inhabitants of protected buildings should seek advice first). Tailor them to catch the sun when it reaches a particular zenith, such as

top: A window on the past.

above: A piece of crocheted cloth acts as a door curtain.

left: Light and shadow create mood and atmosphere.

an east-facing kitchen skylight to trap morning rays. For more hard-to-reach areas such as windowless bathrooms, try installing a 'light tube' (a small bore hole-type skylight with a reflective shaft).

Other ways of magnifying natural light are as easy as cleaning dirty windows: mix one part white distilled vinegar to three parts water for gleaming glass. A well-known trick often used in the days before electricity is to place mirrors opposite windows to bounce the light back into the room. Ensure outdoor surfaces, such as garden walls, are painted in pale colours, to redirect the light indoors. Cut back foliage around windows.

dressing up windows

Use curtains, blinds, and shutters to insulate, keep out prying eyes, and create darkness. Don't go overboard, as windows are one of a room's most expressive features: instead, keep curtains and blinds pared back and simple.

For a natural look, fit Roman blinds, and line for extra insulation. Venetian blinds offer flexible light control, creating emotive, slatted light effects when angled halfway, and also come with added insulation: wood looks best. Slatted wooden shutters, seen on almost every Scandinavian pine lodge and Swiss chalet, are great for small windows as they can be folded right back to let light flood in. Have them tailor-made from recycled woods or scour architectural salvage yards for the genuine article.

For a softer look, gently diffuse daylight with fine fabrics. Woven linen and fine muslin work

well – the light passing through often highlights the textural beauty of the weave. Simply hang or drape a length of fabric over an old broom handle or a wrought iron rod, drawing it back from the window with ties. Other ideas for securing curtains are to sew ribbons in loops to the top of the fabric, then slide onto the pole, or try using café clips to fasten the material to the curtain rod – this way you won't need to puncture delicate fabrics.

With stiffer material (such as canvas or woven grass fabrics), attach it to a curtain rod by making eyelets at regular intervals and lash it to the pole with thin ropes. A more rudimentary way of letting in more light but still keeping a sense of privacy is to take a length of canvas (or leather, suede, or roller blind fabric) and perforate holes to create tiny circles of dappled light. You won't need to create hems and the fabrics are versatile and durable.

Otherwise swap transparent glass for an opaque variety such as sandblasted or frosted glass to create privacy and eschew roving eyes.

left: **An old linen sheet is made into a blind. The light behind it illuminates the weft of the fabric.**

top right: **Wooden shutters create instant darkness and shut out the cold.**

bottom right: **A yachting shackle doubles up as a curtain ring, and brings a simple finish to the top of the curtain.**

artificial light

Artificial light is an essential stand-in for natural light. It creates mood, evokes emotion, and, on a less esoteric level, it's simply functional. Ill-considered lighting is a headache – literally. Unshielded lights, like a naked bulb, strain the eyes, as do thoughtlessly placed light sources with inappropriate coverings. At its worst, artificial light is unsubtle and glaring, emitting a blinding illumination that the human spirit finds tiring, unflattering, and monotonous.

The key to good lighting is to mimic nature. The quality of light throughout the day is constantly changing, so install a system that is versatile and creates interest through different combinations of light and shadow, from bright and dynamic to dimmed and soothing. Avoid single fixed light sources like unkindly pendant lights. Instead, choose uplighters, downlighters, spots, and side lights, positioned or angled to bounce light off walls and ceilings. Always keep in mind the purpose of a room: instil a feeling of relaxation and intimacy in a living room by installing peripheral lighting, while in kitchens, encourage bright uniform lighting for energy and clarity.

First think about the shape of a room, and play light-architect, changing its shape by throwing light onto the ceiling with uplighters to make it appear larger, or try casting soft washes over walls to create a feeling of expansion.

Next take into account the task-specific lighting requirements of that room. For studying and reading, place task lights beside desks or armchairs; for cooking, use spotlights or strip lights over worktops. Anglepoise lights with flexible necks are often a good option if several people of different heights use one particular work area.

Lastly, think about creating atmosphere by, for example, highlighting a sculpture or picture with a downlighter, or installing a dimmer switch, to evoke an emotional response and a feeling of intimacy.

As lighting is one of the most important aspects of any room, consider hiring a design consultant to get a second opinion. Putting down a wiring system is like installing your home's central nervous system: mistakes can be costly, so plan wisely.

Light bulbs matter. For a mellow, yellowy light, opt for incandescent or tungsten-filament bulbs. In the kitchen, brighter, whiter tungsten-halogen bulbs, particularly flattering to food and skin tones, are preferable.

While their lifespan is 13 times greater than incandescent bulbs, fluorescent bulbs seem like an energy-saving grace, but the stark blue-tinge the bulbs emit seems cold-hearted to some. Full-spectrum lamps designed to replicate the spectrum of daylight come recommended by health specialists.

Dress bulbs wisely. Dramatically soften or increase light sources with fittings or shades. Materials such as parchment, paper, silk, and ceramic softly diffuse light, while metal or leather fittings create more directional accents. Ensure light coverings fit within the modern rustic context of clean, unfussy shapes made from natural products: remember details count.

right: A cast iron candelabra is the perfect complement in this cavernous room.

flaming light

Before the first incandescent light bulb was invented by Thomas Edison in 1875, flames from candles or oil lamps were our only sources of light. We are still innately drawn to the dream life of a flame. A candle's light is soft and gentle – we all look beautiful under its gaze. To us, fire-flames are alluring, mesmerizing, and comforting.

Use candle flames for inspiration at night and during the day. Candleholders can be as simple as a decorated tin can (see page 68–69 for details), a sculptural jam jar, or a nook in a stone. Candelabras in dining areas fitted with candles create an intimate atmosphere, but for outdoors, opt for flares, metal hurricane lamps, and storm lanterns. Old junk market finds, such as lanterns, can be easily cleaned up for a modern setting.

left: Textural candles, their organic shape inspired by pebbles on the beach.

far right: Everyday glasses become vessels of light. Create an altar of flame.

right: A rugged storm lantern is the perfect night light in sun lounges, and on decks and patios.

tin lanterns

These pretty lanterns cost almost nothing to make – except a little labour and time – and are safe to use indoors or out.

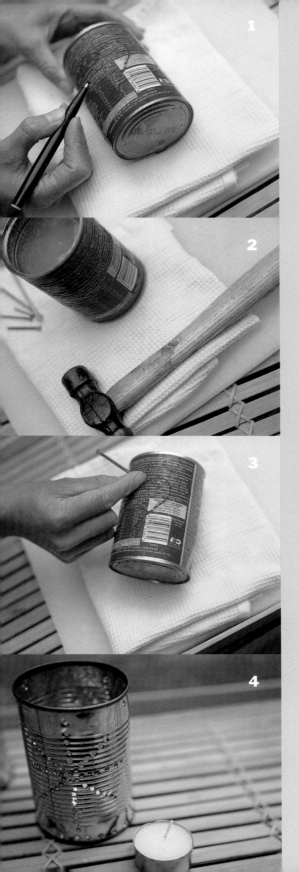

1 Fill a tin can with water and freeze (this will prevent the tin collapsing when you puncture it with a nail). When the water is frozen, remove from freezer and mark out a design of your choice with a marker pen.

2 Place the damp cloth on a chopping board and place the tin on top (the cloth will stop the tin moving around).

3 Using a hammer and nail begin to punch out the design. Continue along the marked design until all the dots are pierced. Vary the design using small and large nails. When you have finished, discard the water.

4 Make two holes opposite each other with the hammer and a nail just beneath the rim. Cut a length of wire for the handle. Thread each end through the holes and wrap the ends around the handle with the pliers. Place a night light inside. You can line the inside of the tin with a piece of coloured acetate for different coloured effects if you prefer.

YOU WILL NEED:
* Tin cans
* Marker pen
* Damp cloth
* Chopping board
* Hammer
* Nails of different sizes
* Very thin galvanized steel wire
* Scissors
* Pair of pliers
* Night lights

heat

Once, at the hub of every house, rural or urban, was a fire. A place for drying damp clothes, thawing frozen bones, or spinning yarns by firelight, the hearth or stove was the emotional and physical heartland. We are instinctively drawn to a flame: it makes us feel warm and secure. When Benjamin Franklin discovered electricity in 1752, he would never have thought that several hundred years later, he would be held accountable for the death of the hearth.

But it's time to rekindle an old flame and revive a tradition. With a new generation of secondary burning stoves and 'smokeless' fuels coupled with a hankering to reconnect with nature's elements, fires are back in modern rustic vogue. Install a fireplace or stove – pieces with past lives salvaged from reclamation yards already tell their own stories. Most old stoves and hearth surrounds are made from rustic's textural elements: wood, stone, wrought iron, brick, and tile. Use an old wooden beam or choose local stone for a mantelpiece.

If it all seems too much, then improvise. Place dozens of lighted candles in one area or an old hearth then cloak the floor with soft, squashy cushions and sheepskins or a faux-fur throw (see pages 78–79 for details), then pull up a sink-into couch or armchair and bask in the blaze of physical and spiritual warmth.

top left: **Seasoned wood, ready to burn.**

bottom left: **For the pure light of a flame without the hassle, light a hearth of candles.**

right: **Salvage the past. This stove, an old 'American light' model, was almost condemned to scrap.**

the practicalities

If you have an old hearth and chimney, before you even think about putting match to wood, have the chimney inspected. Fire smoke will only escape up a chimney if it is hotter and lighter than the surrounding air. A damp, cold draught or blockages caused by soot or loose bricks halt the smoke spiralling upwards, and instead allow toxic smoke and gasses to waft right back into the living room.

Chimneys in older houses may need relining. One technique, 'cast-in-situ' (where concrete is poured into a tailored mould around the existing structure) also adds strength to structurally dubious chimneys. Other indoor-smoke eliminators include proper fire ventilators, such as a flue with a smoke shelf and air damper, and an underfloor duct in front of the fire. Have chimneys professionally swept twice yearly to prevent hazardous tar build-ups.

Bear in mind local regulations. In the United States, the Environmental Protection Agency has introduced controls on all emissions, and in Great Britain, most urban areas are 'smoke controlled'. Generally, 'clean air' laws in built-up areas state that only smokeless solid fuels (such as smokeless coal, gas, or electric fires), or wood stoves with secondary burners (a second stove reignites and burns off solids produced by the original fire, consequently reducing emissions to a minimum) are permitted.

Gas fires have the environmental thumbs up and have thankfully progressed since their 70s heyday as 'living flames'. Now outputting warmth as well as mimicking nature's own blaze, gas fires

are often more fuss-free and better cost-wise than 'real' fires.

Nothing is quite so seductive as the hiss and crackle of burning wood. Attaining the rustic idyll, however, requires forethought – wood fires are labour intensive. When trees are freshly felled, the wood comprises 50 per cent water and consequently requires seasoning (air-drying) for up to twelve months before burning. If the rules of wood seasoning are not strictly adhered to, burning wood deposits highly flammable tar residue on chimney walls, which, unsurprisingly, can spark off chimney fires.

Wood is a renewable resource, but there is no excuse for felling healthy trees. Instead use timber from dead, terminally old, or diseased trees. Coal is perhaps a better alternative: with a high heat content in relation to its weight, it is more efficient than wood, burning evenly and becoming, as the cliché goes, a glowing ember.

What looks hot can be deceptive. About 90 per cent of a fire's heat disappears up the chimney with the smoke, so maximize warmth by installing a convector system. Air is drawn in through a vent at the bottom of the hearth and passes up through a chamber at the back of the fireplace, heating up as it travels. It then crosses through another convection chamber fitted into the roof of the fireplace, and the hot air is expelled into the room.

If heat is your priority, opt for a high-performance airtight stove (fires burn hotter when the door is shut tight), fitted into an existing chimney. For convenience most of these models are built to allow a jet of cold air to run in

left: Build a simple shelter outside where logs can dry out for future flames.

front of the window, ensuring the glass won't be covered in soot, so your view of flickering flames will not be obscured. Central heating systems can also be run off stoves, so once you walk away from the fire, you won't freeze.

warm toes

Underfloor heating isn't a modern concept: the Romans invented it in 60 AD. It's a welcome complement to the staples of the rustic look, because stone, tile, and wood flooring are cold underfoot, but warm up quickly and thrill the soles of the feet. Besides being invisible, underfloor heating is also energy efficient, using resources wisely. Hot air rises, so say the laws of physics, and by generating a gentle, radiant heat at floor level, the warm air doesn't escape quickly. And instead of just coming from one source, underfloor heat evenly distributes warmth over a wide area. Use in large living rooms and bathrooms, or wherever you are likely to be barefoot.

Most systems are 'wet' (hot water is pumped underneath the floor) operating off a gas central heating system: one boiler can heat both the radiators and the underfloor grid of pipes. 'Dry' systems, running off electricity, are not as cost-efficient, but have the same warm-toed effect.

left: **A small corner stove takes the chill out of the air.**

right: **A fire appeals to our innate primal nature, effusing rooms with congeniality and warmth.**

below: **This model almost looks like a pet. Stoke and it will purr with heat.**

radiant radiators

Part of the charm of rustic is reconnecting with old things. Compared with chunky, solid radiators, modern models somehow don't look *right* in this context (unless they are subtle, like convector or plinth heaters). Delve around reclamation and salvage yards to resurrect classic, timeless styles, but purchase old radiators ready renovated as shot-blasting, renewing air vents, and pressure testing is costly – leave it to experts.

harness the sun

Sun energy is free. As the sun warms the earth, so the day star can channel heat indoors. Based on the principles of solar radiation, retention, storage, and circulation, the two most popular sun-propelled systems available are based on employing solar panels on roofs and sun-facing walls. One converts sunshine into electricity, the other uses the heat to warm up water, storing it in water tanks or rock beds, to be distributed by pipes and ducts as required.

How much these systems produce is entirely dependent on the amount of solar energy you receive, hence if you live in unreliable climes, sun-reliant methods are best used in combination with a fail-proof arrangement.

insulate

Retain heat. Draught-proof all walls and window linings. In medieval times, decorators discovered thick curtains and fabrics assisted in heat retention – the offshoot was a wealth of tapestry art. Our interpretation is heavy curtains: however, seek out antique bedspreads or rugs for classic style.

left: Modern radiators pale in comparison to beautiful old stalwarts. Purchase these from second-hand shops or salvage yards.

right: Stay warm in winter with woollen throws and heavy curtains, or even a luxurious fake-fur blanket.

fur throw

Curl up beside the fire with this sumptuous throw, or add an extra layer to your bed for wintry warmth.

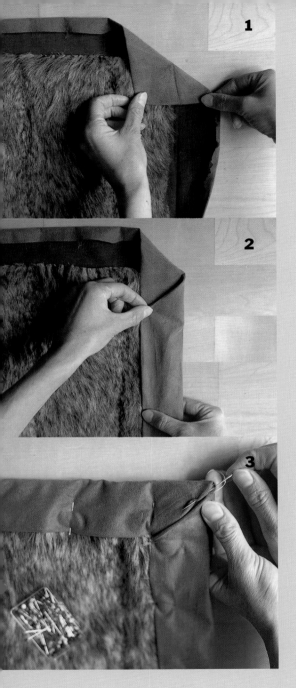

1 Place the fake fur in the centre of the suede, right sides facing outwards. Pin and tack. Fold the raw edge of the suede over 2cm / $\frac{3}{4}$ in and press. Taking each corner in turn, fold the corner of the suede over the fur fabric so that the fold encloses the tip of the fur.

2 Take the two outer corners of the triangle and fold in toward each other so that the edges touch. You will now have a perfect mitred corner. Pin in place. Fold the sides of the suede over the fur and pin in place.

3 With a needle and thread, blind stitch the two edges of the corner together, by making small invisible stitches between the folds. Place the sewing machine foot about 1cm / $\frac{1}{2}$ in from the edge of the suede and machine stitch all the way round the throw. Remove the pins and tacking threads, and press.

YOU WILL NEED:
* Approximately 2.5m/2½yd square of fake fur
* Equal amount of fake suede, but add on 7cm/3in fold allowance
* Sewing machine
* Sewing kit
* Iron

scent

Our noses were originally the tools by which we lived and died. Our nostrils helped us find sustenance, discern the difference between good and stale food, and kept us out of danger – we literally 'smelt' fear. Still innately we work off this primal instinct when we choose a mate. Despite our attempts to attract the opposite sex with perfumes, we are still magnetized to some body odours, while others we find repugnant.

The word 'modern' seems disconnected from that of 'smell'. We, the human animal, can detect over 10,000 aromas, but in our increasingly sanitized, deodorized environments, our olfactory sense has been castrated. The air we breathe is 'conditioned', our washing is machine-spun not sun dried, our perfumes, airfresheners, and laundry sprays are made from synthetic imitations of plants, a trite imitation of the *real* thing.

Every culture has recognized the pleasures and benefits of natural fragrances. Lavender was once the medieval housewife's favourite strewing herb, placed in linen cupboards to scent clothes, and hung in the corners of the room to keep away flies, mosquitoes, and the plague. Dandelions were the 'country clock', opening at five in the morning and closing at eight in the evening, while garlic was used to ward off evil spirits. Pot pourris, pomanders, and incense were placed or burnt in homes and churches to garnish a room's aroma.

left: A few fresh flowers cut from the garden carry a subtle fragrance.

top right: Freshly cut lemons release an uplifting, refreshing scent.

bottom right: Banish artificial room fragrances and instil scents of nature.

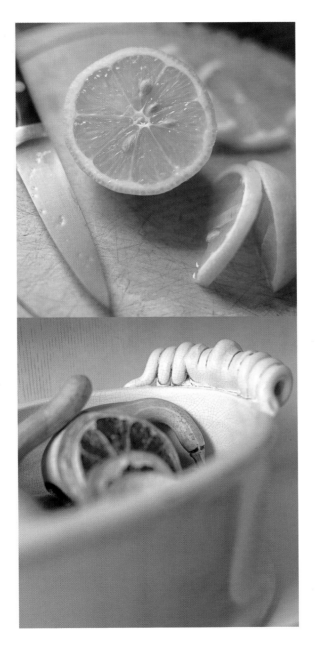

grow your own

Nature's own perfumes are inimitable. There is no excuse, even in a concrete-clad cityscape, for not bringing flowers and plants inside. Grow herbs such as peppermint, thyme, lemon balm, lavender, basil, parsley, and rosemary in window boxes and tubs just outside the back door, or on little pots along the windowsill, all of which make delicious additions to cooking dishes. If your greenfinger has grim-reaping tendencies, opt for plants such as lavender and rosemary, which thrive in arid soil. For heady fragrances, buy jasmine, lilies, and roses for the home; or if you work late, choose honeysuckle and night scented stock which release their perfume under the disguise of nightfall.

Once your crops are flourishing, harvest and use them. Add fresh basil to salads, rosemary to lamb dishes, parsley (with a knob of butter) to potatoes.

Make teas from dried flowers or freshly cut herbs. 'Moroccan tea' is highly regarded throughout the Arabic world as an 'internal refresher': to aid digestion, take two tablespoons of green tea, add two pints of boiling water, a cupful of fresh mint and brew together in a teapot. Let the pot sit for about five minutes, then pour, sugaring to taste if needed. Before sipping, inhale the divine scent of fresh hot mint. A brilliant pick-me-up is rosemary tea. Chop up sprigs of rosemary, then pour over boiling-hot water. Again wait for the flavours to become empowered. Before drinking, breathe in its more pungent odour – headaches will dissipate and clarity of thought will ensue.

top left: **An indoor herb garden for cooking, tea-making, or to simply appreciate. Just add water.**

bottom left: **Moroccan mint tea. Inhale the refreshing scent, before sipping slowly.**

To extend the shelf life of herbs and flowers, dry them out and use them in herb bags, sachets, pot pourris, and soaps. Hang fragrant herb bags in the wardrobe, or place in your drawers to add a light floral bouquet to your clothes. The easiest way to dry flowers is to hang them upside down in a dark place. For premium long-lasting scents and looks, first ensure flowers and herbs are completely dry when picked; moisture invariably turns them brown or mouldy. Store the dried stems in a cardboard box in a dark dry place, taking care not to pack too many into a single box, thereby squashing and exhausting the plants, then use as required.

right: Lavender for calming and relaxing. Just a few stems in a jug or vase brightens up a room with their soft lilac hue and gentle fragrance.

essential oils

With alternative medicine has come an interest in the healing properties of plants and their scents. 'Aromatherapy' was a word first coined by Renée Maurice Gattefosse, a French chemist, who was a perfumer in the 1920s. He burnt his arm and, with no cold water nearby, plunged it into a vat of lavender oil. Over the next couple of days, it healed extraordinarily quickly. Fascinated, he set about dedicating the rest of his life to researching the healing properties of plants.

From his seminal work came essential oils, produced from flower petals, gums, leaves, stalks, seeds, and roots – there are now over 300 aromas to choose from.

Essential oils work by infiltrating the body through the pores (by bathing or through massage), or by scent (carried on steam or vapour), which once inhaled through the nose is diffused into the lungs and distributed around the body.

When choosing scents, aromatherapists advocate allowing your nostrils to instinctively guide you to the smell your body requires. Scents such as rose relieve stress and depression, while other scents such as sandalwood make us feel solid and secure. In the winter, opt for warming smells such as musk, amber, vanilla, and sandalwood; for cooling smells choose lavender, rose, or rosemary.

Use the oils in a burner, sprinkle on pillow slips, spray around the house using a vaporizer of purified water and essential oil, or make your own scented candles (see pages 86–87 for details) to burn and release their subtle aroma.

top left: The essential
ingredient for oils is a burner.
Add half a dozen drops to the
water in the bowl and light a
night light underneath.

bottom left: Burning incense
has a richly pungent aroma.
Light a joss stick to unwind
in the evening.

right: Pull the curtains back,
open the window wide, and let
natural scents and precious
oxygen waft indoors.

fresh air

Let in air. Besides scenting your home from the
inside, ventilate with pure, natural oxygen. Stale
air and indoor pollutants stop us fully
functioning. To ensure good quality air in your
home, and create a naturally scented, odour-free
air space, remove and reduce all artificial smells:
use herbal soaps, furniture creams, and safe,
non-polluting cleaning fluids where possible,
and ventilate regularly, including in the depths
of winter.

Even in an urban environment, 'rustic'
scents – the smell of the rain on the pavement,
a whiff of damp leaves – convey a sense of the
season, and keep us in touch with the time of
day. Create a cross flow between windows, letting
out stale air and revitalizing rooms with fresh air.
And then inhale.

scented candles

As they burn, the candles release a soft lavender fragrance to gently relax and soothe.

modern rustic

1 Put the wax into the upper compartment of a double boiler. Fill the outer compartment with water and heat to a low boil (do not let the water spit as it can spoil the wax if they come into contact). Allow the wax to melt and heat to 85°C/180°F, monitoring the temperature closely with the thermometer.

2 Thread the wick through the candle mould. Secure the bottom around the stick. Dip the top end into the melted wax (this prevents the mould seal from clogging the wick), and secure with the mould seal. Following the manufacturer's instructions, dissolve the dye in a separate double boiler. The dye disc has to be dissolved in stearin; as a rough guide use 10 per cent stearin to the amount of wax to be coloured. Don't overheat the dye as it spoils easily. When dissolved, add the dye to the wax mixture, keeping the temperature of the wax constant. Add a few drops of lavender oil (or chosen fragrance). Pour two-thirds of the heated wax into the mould, keeping the remainder at the constant temperature of 85°C/180°F.

3 Place the mould in a bucket, and pour in water up to the level of the wax. Place a weight on top of the mould to hold it steady. Let the wax cool for about 3–5 minutes until the mixture thickens: it will gain opacity. Add lavender seeds. See whether they settle on the top. Then top up with the remaining third of the wax and place back in the bucket to cool.

4 After another 15 minutes check the mould to see if a well has appeared in the surface of the centre of the wax. If so remove the candle from the water bath, break the surface with a needle, and top off with hot wax again. You may need to do this several times before the candle cools properly. When cool, just tap gently on the bottom of the mould and pull out the candle by tugging on the stick. If it doesn't come out first time put the candle in the fridge for a few hours and try again. To finish off, trim the wicks and light.

YOU WILL NEED:
To make one candle measuring 16 x 6 x 6cm/6½ x 2½ x 2½ in

* 24 level tbsp of refined beaded paraffin wax
* A couple of double boilers or old saucepans
* Jam-making thermometer
* Wooden spoon
* 10–25cm/8–10in wick string
* Candle mould 16 x 6 x 6cm/ 6½ x 2½ x 2½in
* Lollipop or stick
* Mould seal
* Dye discs
* Stearin (a necessary additive for dye)
* Perfumed lavender oil (specially designed for candles)
* Bucket
* Large pebble or similar heavy object to act as weight
* Dried lavender seeds
* Needle

detail

Detail is a house's personal signature. It's the little things that denote the difference between home and hotel, which explains why we never feel settled in a rented room – even for a night – until our possessions are strewn about. Without detail, a place simply has no spirit – it feels unfurnished. Perhaps it is why minimalism has been abandoned: we simply hunger for things around us. They tell us who we are, what we love, tell stories, evoke wit and joy, and provoke memories. Objects reveal our taste, past, and humour, acting as messengers of sensuality and beauty.

There are two types of details: those that are functional and those that act as decoration. When considering function, Ilse Crawford so aptly observes in *Sensual Home*, that 'No house ever feels truly harmonious unless the details are right. A doorknob is the handshake of a house. If the doorknobs are awkward to hold, if light switches are crude and intrusive, if bath taps refuse to turn smoothly or if a window sticks wilfully in its frame – the integrity of our home and the pleasure we ought to gain from living in it is undermined.'

left: **Modern rustic is also about celebrating your own past, keeping the careworn, cherished objects of your life around you.**

top right: **Knock on wood – with style.**

middle right: **An unexpected slice of nature.**

bottom right: **The mottled hues of a collection of pebbles.**

modern rustic

function first

Pay attention to practical detail. Country essentials such as generously proportioned bread bins, solid bread boards, voluminous watering cans, wooden pegs, and chunky scissors are all designed for functionality and durability. Other 'rural essentials' – glass jars and jam pots designed for endless batches of stewing fruits and spreads, and family heirlooms sturdy enough to be passed down from generation to generation – are now surfacing in antique shops, second-hand stores, flea markets, and junk shops. Go scouting for these brilliant basics, or fossik around stores to uncover a modern equivalent with country virtues of solidity and reliability.

Other daily dining staples such as plates, teacups, glasses, cutlery, and cooking pots and casserole dishes also regularly make a star appearance at markets and car boot sales. Instead of buying brand new plates, purchase pre-loved ones, picking out a selection by matching them via colour or pattern. Old china cups also extol a dainty beauty hard to find in modern versions. Solid-in-the-hand yet delicate-to-look-at antique silver cutlery is another treasure to snap up for luxurious dining.

For vases and display pots, opt for organic, sculptural lines, and curvy slimline shapes made by the human hand. Things that show a connection between maker and material are more alluring than those off a production line.

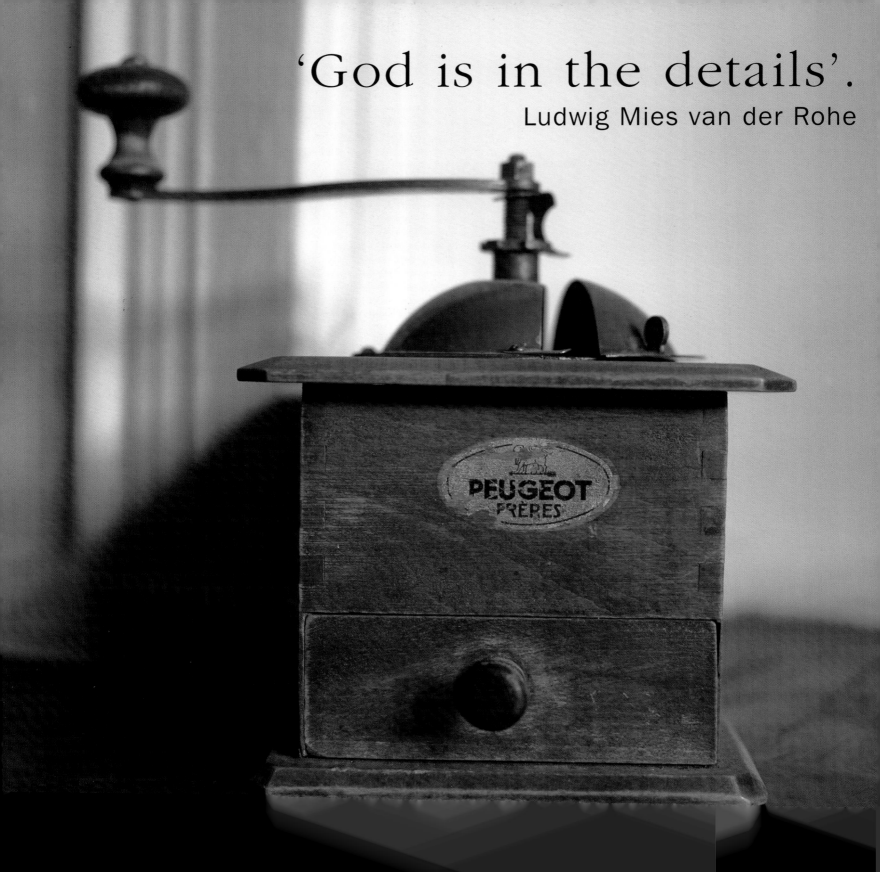

'God is in the details'.
Ludwig Mies van der Rohe

objects of expression

Decoration must provoke a response. It can make us smile, feel nostalgic, surprise or ground us. The real essence of decoration is to surround yourself with things you feel passionate about. Small slices of memorabilia – pictures of ancestors, a drawing by a child friend, a piece of hand-hewn pottery, a postcard from an old lover – are a treasury of tales, connecting us visually and emotionally with the people who mean something to us.

Make your bathroom a photo gallery, create a mantelpiece altar, or string up a piece of wire and clip on mementoes.

top right: For an element of surprise, just use a single leaf or a duo of sculptural stems in a vase to captivate the eye.

middle right: Pumpkins are not just for Halloween, they're funky objects too.

bottom right: Sprinkle rose petals around an open fireplace.

When we look at a piece of nature, a single thought reflex connects us with the earth. The well trodden path of bringing inside the *joie de vivre* of the country is to buy bundles of flowers and pot plants. But, don't just stick to stylized floral arrangements. Over the centuries posies and bunches of flowers have become too predictable. Instead try something new: scatter rose petals around a hearth, stack twigs on top of one another, or just use two seed pod stems instead of a posy. 'Arrange' the unexpected.

Some of the earth's best ornaments cost nothing. Dry out squashes, pumpkins, and butternuts in a darkened space and showcase in a pale enamelled bowl. Or hang bunches of roses up in a row to dry, pitching their papery soft colours against one another.

Next time you go beachcombing or tramping in the countryside, search out opulent shells, pebbles in a range of mottled hues, jewels of broken glass bottles, colourful leaves, and arrange in small clusters.

Immortalize nature once you've found it. Make it into prints (see pages 96–97 for details), or glue pieces onto jewellery boxes. And take a child with you, they have an innate sense of shape and colour.

Don't confuse detail with clutter. Let large spaces, such as living rooms, breathe easily, but beside an expanse of sofa, place an altar of stones and a picture. Look for areas where detail leads to surprise: a cluster of stone-like candles on a window ledge; a knot of beach shells in the bathroom; a picture of a revered great-grandfather on a wall. Innovate and experiment.

nature paper prints

Engage solar energy and capture nature's shapes and patterns on sun sensitive paper.

1 Make up a design for your nature print from your collection of *objets trouvés*.

2 When you are happy with your design, place the items on sun sensitive paper in direct sunlight. If necessary weight them down by placing a glass on top. Be very careful not to expose the sun sensitive paper to light before use. Wait until you are ready, then take it out of the box at the last minute. Leave in the sun for 5–8 minutes until the paper turns almost white. Then transfer to the shade, and place the paper in a water bath for approximately 5 minutes. Watch the colour fade and reappear. Dry the paper on a flat surface – the paper will darken.

3 Cut two pieces of cardboard the same size as the hardboard. On the first piece, mark a border with the pencil and ruler. Cut along the marked line with a craft knife or scalpel and remove the central section. This will give you a picture frame. Place the nature print in the centre of the second piece of cardboard. On the reverse of the hardboard score a line 2cm/ ¾ in in from the outside edge around all four sides.

4 Sandwich the picture mount and frame between the hardboard and glass and secure with picture clips, which will snap into place along the scored line on the reverse of the hardboard.

YOU WILL NEED:
* Objets trouvés (leaves, grasses, shells, flower heads, seeds)
* Sun sensitive paper (available from craft shops)
* Glass to act as a weight
* Old washing up bowl to act as a water bath
* Piece of hardboard cut to chosen size
* Sheet of cardboard
* Metal ruler and pencil
* Scissors
* Craft knife or scalpel
* Glass cut to chosen size
* Four picture clips

rustic living

bathing

Cleanliness is next to Godliness. So said the prudish Victorians, advising young girls to shut their eyes and not look at their bodies when towelling themselves down. The Victorians equated the pleasures of the tub with sinfulness: revelling in a long, hot bath was considered licentious, libidinous behaviour, almost certain to lead the devout Christian astray. Consequently, in the nineteenth century only classy brothels and grand hotels had decent large bathing facilities.

Other cultures have not been quite so sanctimonious. In Roman times the bath masqueraded as political hotbed, a place to exchange gossip and socialize. Historians have speculated that the extortionate time spent in the baths, coupled with poisoning delivered via lead pipes, probably contributed to Rome's downfall.

Some cultures still place a huge importance on the communal bath. A convoluted metamorphosis of the Roman bath has now become the Arabic hammam, often attached to mosques, so doubling as a place for spiritual contemplation as well as socializing.

In Finnish culture, the sauna is sacred. And although there are only about five million people in Finland, there are over two million sweat lodges. In fact, saunas are so important to the Finns, the sauna is often erected before the house. The enclosure is a communal sanctuary

top left: Exfoliate and scrub the body with a pumice-stone and a natural sponge before stepping into the bath.

bottom left: Eschew ersatz-scented soaps. Opt instead for natural body washes made from plant extracts and vegetable oils.

right: Pure relaxation. A Japanese tradition is to bathe with a view out onto a garden, allowing the bather to reconnect with the natural world.

for physical and mental rejuvenation, but no heated conversations or family tiffs are permitted. Perhaps the sauna's reverence comes from its past life as a sanctuary where women gave birth: these pinewood safe harbours were one of the few places with a well-stocked supply of hot water.

In Japan, where there are over 20,000 natural springs, bathing is considered a holistic experience, a scrubbing out of both body and mind. Baths or *onsen* are often sited in remote, rustic places, high up in the mountains surrounded by sweet-scented cedar and cypress forests.

In modern Western culture, bathing has become one of our prized and most fiercely defended rituals. For most of us it is still a private love affair (a hangover from the Victorian era) and one we cherish, for it is one of the few times in the day when we are completely alone. Unlike the repressive Victorians, we have become bathing zealots, using water as much to refresh and relax as to cleanse our bodies. If it is one of our daily rituals, why not make it a pleasurable experience – and a rustic one?

left: A modern twist on the bateau bath. Clawed feet are replaced with sleek warm wood. Suddenly it's not just a tub, it's a sculpture.

bathroom design

When planning the layout of a new home, remember that the bathroom doesn't need to be tucked away in the smallest room of the house. If possible, choose a large room and transform it into one in which you would enjoy spending time, with ample space for showering, bathing, dressing, and storage—design the layout with designated areas for each activity.

Separating the bath and shower is a design concept the Japanese would agree with. The Japanese consider the Western notion of cleansing and bathing in the same tub unhygienic and defeatist. They would never dream of stepping into a bath unless their bodies were thoroughly cleansed and scrubbed first. Bathers who have tried this practical tradition rarely look back.

In bathroom design, introducing a watertight tiled floor that slopes toward a central drainage system will allow water to drain off wet areas. Mosaic tiles work well in this kind of environment—for safety reasons, ensure they are nonslip.

When choosing a bath, size counts. A bath should be spacious enough to wallow in. Ensure it is deep so that your body is buoyant and weightless, and your neck is fully supported. Try before you buy—yes, lie in it! Think about how it is going to work with the design of your bathroom—do you want it to take center stage, or be positioned against the wall?

Don't be constrained by traditional sites for the bath—it can be equally at home in the bedroom, an idea innovated by the revolutionary

top left: To reach those important little places, or to wash without wetting your hair, opt for a detachable hand-held shower head.

bottom left: Classic style fittings never date. Why? Their design is functional as well as aesthetic.

modernist Le Corbusier whose bathroom-cum-bedroom at the Villa Savoye (1928–31) involved a boxed-off bathing area in a traditional bedroom suite. Check plumbing details with an expert before you embark on this option.

For the rustic ultimate go for a wooden bath. As well as being extremely sensuous to the touch, wooden tubs also retain the heat, unlike pressed steel baths, which can quickly lose it. Opt for tropical woods such as iroko, merabau, cedar, and rubber woods, as these all possess inherent water-repellent and antibacterial properties. Be eco-conscious, however, and purchase recycled woods from salvage companies.

To clean this type of bath, don't use detergents as they strip the wood of its natural oils: buy wood soap instead. Most wooden baths have to be tailor-made to suit your bathroom; scout interiors magazines or ask bathroom specialists for recommended fitters.

With furnishings and fittings, look for country-sized portions. Large roseheads (shower heads), double-ended reproduction baths, and chunky chrome-plated pillar taps are best.

To source these, head to architectural salvage yards, but beware, however, as there may be extra costs in restoring pieces to top-notch condition.

Re-enamelling and re-firing a French bateau bath often costs as much as the bath itself. Modern taps and waste traps will not fit period baths and basins, so buy models in tandem with the tub. If you often bathe with a companion, choose models with taps in the middle for comfortable bathing *á deux*.

top right: **A modern sink is evocative of a traditional wash bowl, and is complemented by sleek fittings.**

bottom right: **Think ergonomics. Keep everything within easy reach. This scuffed enamel soap dish also adds a little rustic charm.**

If baths are for wallowing and dreaming, so showers refresh and invigorate. They are more energy efficient than baths, although if your water jet is not entirely satisfactory, they can be quite a dreary experience. Rectify the situation with a booster pump or power shower (which uses 50 per cent more water than a conventional shower) to provide a decent blast.

If your plumbing allows you to have a watertight floor, section off a corner area with panes of glass, making sure it has its own drainage site, and have a sliding or push-out glass door. Try to avoid soggy plastic or nylon shower curtains.

To create a rustic look in the bathroom, cloak the walls and floor in nature's materials. For 'wet' areas use ceramic, non-slip tiles, slate, or marble. Paint walls with a microporous coating (which allows them to breathe), or finish in an aromatic wood cladding, such as Japanese cypress and cedar, or breathable untreated cork.

Think windows. If you have a windowless bathroom, see if you can knock out a skylight to let in natural light and create extra ventilation. Put up wooden slatted blinds and shutters at the windows rather than curtains, which can spoil with damp.

pure indulgence

Having an outdoor or indoor private Jacuzzi and sauna is like owning your own health spa, although Jacuzzis are expensive to run and energy consuming. Hot water, passed through pressurized jets, is mixed with air, providing a micromassage.

The health benefits outweigh the cost, however, as the water stimulates the skin, drawing out body toxins, and soothing and reviving aching muscles.

Saunas are a more economical choice. Traditionally, they are pinewood log cabins, centred around a stove topped off with several hard peridotite rocks (a type of granite). By ladling water onto the red-hot stones, dry air becomes instantaneously moist, stimulating the skin and nervous system. A nearby shower for cooling down is essential. To install either a Jacuzzi or sauna, consult an expert for planning and fitting advice.

a recipe for outdoor bathing

Buy an old porcelain bath from an architectural salvage yard (preferably with legs) and put it in the backyard. Fill with collected rainwater and start a woodfire underneath. Wait for about an hour, stoking the fire regularly until the water is deliciously hot, and then let the wood fire burn down to a smoulder. Place a smooth wooden board underneath your bottom if necessary (it may be too hot to sit in otherwise), then hop in. Luxuriate under the sky.

Outdoor bathing and showering is rustic at its rawest. For a quick pre-dinner shower in hot climes, section off an unused sunny garden spot with good drainage, lay down slatted wooden beams underfoot, and erect wooden screens (for modesty). Create a system for collecting rain water and attach a shower head below. If you prefer, rig up a solar panel system (available from outdoor adventure stores).

right: Keep accessories pure and natural, such as a slatted cedar wood bath mat.

below: Rustic details add earthiness to otherwise clinical bathroom settings. A recycled oak beam becomes a shelf to stow towels and face cloths.

accessories

For accessories choose things with a charisma *au naturel*. Linen and cotton towels are best against the skin: dry them out on the line rather than in the tumble dryer to instil a breath of summer freshness into your bathroom. Introduce springy towelling bath mats, or complement your wooden bath with a mat made of scented cedar wood. Buy sea sponges to wash with, and bristle brushes to scuff off dead skin cells. Use soaps made from natural plant extracts, or better still, make you own (see pages 110–111 for details).

Scented baths date back to the bathoholic Romans, who once used lavender to perfume their baths. *Lavare*, from which the word lavender is derived, means 'to wash'. In a bath, herbs or oils infiltrate the body through the pores or are carried in the steam and inhaled through the nose, diffused into the lungs, and distributed throughout the entire body.

For herbal infusions, hang a muslin bag filled with fresh or dried herbs under a hot, running tap, letting the bath fill up slowly, or add strong, potent infusions to the water, leaving them to soak for at least 15–30 minutes before stepping into the bath.

For a forest-scented, uplifting bath, try soaking with pouches of fresh pine branch tips; to relax, douse with infusions of camomile flowers; or to invigorate and refresh, immerse yourself in water with bags of freshly-picked rosemary stems.

Oils are less fuss. Either pour a few drops directly into the water, or make a bath oil using sweet almond, avocado, or vitamin-E rich wheatgerm oil to enrich the skin, as a base.

Take an Eastern approach to bathing. Vigorously exfoliate your body with a pumice-stone, and a loofah, bath glove, or brush, and rinse thoroughly before stepping into a piping hot perfumed bath. Steamy hot water releases and opens the pores of the skin, drawing out toxins and aiding sluggish circulation. To prevent pores clogging up, 'close' them by finishing with a cold shower. While your skin is still damp, apply a body moisturiser to replenish depleted body oils.

Once you've introduced natural materials and fragrances into the bathroom, don't pollute it by cleaning with bleaches and synthetic deodorants. Use tea tree oil as a natural disinfectant; it kills germs and has a tangy, zesty smell.

Mixing one part white distilled vinegar to three parts water will give you a good general cleaner, particularly useful for washing tiles and removing limescale. Tougher jobs require a teaspoon of borax and washing soda, two tablespoons of vinegar, and two cups of hot water in a spray bottle.

left: Smell the scents of summer in linen dried in sweet fresh air.

handmade soap

An oatmeal and lemon balm soap exfoliates the skin and leaves it feeling soft with a gentle tangy scent.

1 Grease the moulds and set to one side. Weigh out all the base fats, oils, and beeswax, and place them in an old cooking pot. Heat the mixture gently until melted, then turn off the heat and wait until the oils reach approximately 54.4°C/130°F, stirring occasionally with a spatula.

2 Wearing rubber gloves and goggles, weigh out the sodium hydroxide. Following the instructions on the sodium hydroxide package, measure out the correct amount of water and heat in another old cooking pot until the water is just beginning to boil. Remove from the heat and stir in the sodium hydroxide granules. Leave until the temperature drops to about 54.4°C/130°F. At this stage it is important not to inhale the fumes and to wear eye and hand protection.

3 Add to the melted oils, stirring constantly until the mixture thickens to a caramel sauce-like consistency. It is ready when you can do a 'trace' test: run some mixture off the back of a spoon and it will leave a trace line on the surface of the mixture. At this stage, add the lemon and clary sage essential oils and the oatmeal, and stir to combine.

4 Pour the mixture into the greased mould, scraping it off the sides of the bowl with a spatula. Cover with a towel and leave for 24 hours or until it has set. Then, wearing rubber gloves, turn the soap out of the mould and cut it into shapes with a sharp knife. Cover the soap again with a fresh towel to insulate and leave to cure at room temperature for at least a month before use.

YOU WILL NEED:
* Tin or plastic container for mould
* Non-stick cooking spray (for greasing moulds)
* 680g/24oz vegetable fat (shortening)
* 227g/8oz coconut oil
* 57g/2oz beeswax
* Kitchen scales
* Measuring jug and spoons
* Large stainless steel pots
* Two plastic spatulas
* Two glass sugar thermometers (range from below 38°C/100°F and up to at least 98°C/200°F
* Rubber gloves
* Protective eye goggles
* 142g/5oz sodium hydroxide (caustic soda/lye)
* Stainless steel ladle
* 10g/2tsp lemon essential oil
* 10g/2tsp clary sage
* 85g/3oz oatmeal
* Towels
* Sharp knife

Note: You can buy sodium hydroxide (also known as caustic soda or lye) from chemists or builders' merchants. Ensure it is 100 per cent pure. Always store in an airtight container to protect it from damp and only handle with rubber gloves. Make sure you throw away the cloths you use to clean up spilt soap, as they will be caustic.

eating

the modern rustic kitchen

Badger's kitchen in Kenneth Grahame's *Wind in the Willows*, is the exemplar of a rustic idyll. '…a large fire-lit kitchen. The floor was well-worn red brick and on the wide hearth burnt a fire of logs…. Rows of spotless plates winked from the shelves of the dresser at the far end of the room, and from the rafters overhead hung hams, bundles of dried herbs, nets of onions and baskets of eggs'.

This traditional farmhouse kitchen, exuding colour, abundance, and hygiene without sterility, should be modern rustic's role model. But let's not forget Mrs Badger. The traditional cookhouse meant ceaseless cleaning, chopping, polishing, firewood fetching, hand-washing, and ensuring constant water supplies – not to forget baking, grilling, frying, stewing, pickling, plucking, and steaming. That's where twentieth-century technology such as electric ovens, dishwashers, capacious refrigerators, microwaves, freezers, blenders, and steamers, becomes as indispensable as sliced bread. The perfect rustic kitchen is a marriage of both worlds.

The modern must-haves of a traditional kitchen include ample storage and preparation space, hard-wearing natural surfaces, ventilation, recycled waste facilities, and durable utensils. In the kitchens of old, a constant influx of fresh produce equalled roomy, well-ventilated storage

left: The traditional farmhouse kitchen, where an easy, informal, benevolently large table acts as a magnet for people and activities.

right: Early kitchen equipment designs have proved to be enduring, and are still selected over their modern cousins.

left: **Good ergonomics: a butcher's block for chopping meats and vegetables is within arm's reach of the stove.**

spaces, like pantries and food safes. With endless foot traffic, hard-working stone or wood floors were essential, as were hardy worktops.

Other features included double sinks (one for preparing vegetables, the other for washing up), a butcher's block for chopping, a marble board for pastry making, and a luxuriously large kitchen table for communal meals. Items such as glass jars were reused; organic waste was recycled as compost. Pots, pans, and cooking dishes were made from cast iron, earthenware, glass, and steel. Utilitarian and uncomplicated were the traditional kitchen's buzzwords.

In a modern kitchen where fresh produce is the focus, all these traditional features remain pertinent. Function and layout were – and still should be – centred around the main activities of storing, preparing, cooking, and feasting.

function and design

One of the initial design decisions for the kitchen should be based on the overall plan of the house, focusing on the roles of the rooms. Do you use your dining room everyday, or does it often sit empty? Do you prefer the informality of eating in the kitchen? Does the kitchen double up as a space for homework and study?

If your dining room is only used once a week, think about amalgamating the space with the kitchen, knocking through walls to make a generously-sized living area for cooking, eating, socializing, and working. With an extended informal dining area, the modern kitchen becomes more flexible, accommodating various home-related activities, which flow in and out of it like a tide throughout the day. Another option is to switch a small kitchen with a larger lounge to make a family area.

Although the kitchen's main roles of cooking, storing, and preparing food drive its fundamental layout, if you've established that dining and breakfasting are also part of its function, designate specific areas for these other activities, ensuring movement around the kitchen is not impaired. Larger spaces make planning easy, although fitting dining areas into small spaces is still possible with ingenious tricks such as flip-down tables or breakfast bars with slender barstools.

Measure up your kitchen, deciding where to position the main sites of activity. Design experts recommend that the hob, sink, and preparation area should form a working triangle. Over the last few decades two basic layouts – the U-shape and the L-shape – have emerged as the two most

top right: **For a roomy refrigerator, look for the streamlined curves of a 50s' design to sit amicably alongside other robust pieces of furniture.**

bottom right: **Wooden worktops have warm, tactile qualities. Research has shown that the natural acidity of wood inhibits bacterial growth.**

ergonomic designs, so think how these can be integrated into your layout plans.

The traditional rustic kitchen was furnished with freestanding units, such as dressers and larders, which could be moved to facilitate cleaning. Many kitchen designs nowadays provide a choice of fitted and freestanding units to allow you to make up an informal kitchen of your choice, with a range of styles in units, door fronts, and handles, to match the size and shape of your room.

If the kitchen is the heart of the home, a good worktop is its pulse. Worktops have to be resilient, functional, and handsome. Ensure that worktops sit at waist-height, so that when preparing food, your back is never strained.

There is a range of surface options to choose from; all have their pros and cons. Granite is the toughest of worktop surfaces, but comes with a price-tag to suit. Slate and limestone are porous and liable to stain, so use a wooden chopping board to compensate. Marble also marks, but is great for making the perfect pastry. Wood requires maintenance – only hardwoods, such as maple, beech, or cherry should be used (softwoods don't last the distance). Stainless steel, the darling of today's interiors, easily becomes scratched and smeared, but is extremely durable. Tiles make excellent splashbacks, although only thick tiles should ever be used on worktops as thin ones have a tendency to break.

And keep worktops clear: never swamp them with gadgets. They should be a generous arm's length in width to relieve preparation congestion and allow ample room for essential appliances

top left: **Food, glorious food. Glass storage jars enable food to be displayed rather than tucked out of sight.**

bottom left: **Allow fresh groceries to breathe in wicker baskets. Stow close to the stove for easy access.**

such as the kettle and toaster. Keep crockery, food, and cookware out of the way, but within easy reach. Hang utensils and pans on a hanging rail, store plates in a rack over the sink or draining board where they can easily drip dry, and use a peg rail for frequently used items.

Most of us do not have the space for a pantry, but a food cupboard sited against a cool external wall with several vents acts as a good alternative. With the advent of packaged meals and once-a-week supermarket shopping, we've been lulled into the habit of putting everything in the refrigerator, but in many cases this isn't necessary. Fresh produce does not need to be stored there, and is often better kept in dark, cool areas, such as storage drawers or baskets (made from wicker and wood).

One of the most important considerations in any style of kitchen is the floor, which will inevitably be bombarded with grease, water, heat, and heavy appliances. Traditional coverings – stone, tiles, and wood – are by far the soundest investments, although cork and linoleum are also tough, low-maintenance options. Whatever you choose, make sure it is non-slip and easy to clean.

Lighting is another vital consideration in a kitchen, and one that is often overlooked. Task lighting, such as spotlights, or recessed strip lights over work surfaces are essential; ambient and decorative lighting is more appropriate over eating areas.

In small kitchens, make good use of wall space with mounted units, taking care to keep a reasonable gap between the bottom of the unit

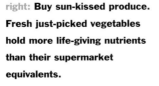
right: **Buy sun-kissed produce. Fresh just-picked vegetables hold more life-giving nutrients than their supermarket equivalents.**

left: **This eight-sided coffee pot is a reproduction of a model designed in 1930 by Alfonso and Renato Bialetti.**

and the work surface. Transparent doors or open shelving can create an illusion of space. Consider also installing a central island unit, which can function as table, storage, and worktop.

Don't be seduced by high technology. Invest instead in brilliant, high quality basics – a large razor-sharp knife, a pair of salad scissors, a sturdy garlic crusher, earthenware pots, and stainless-steel pans.

Above all, instil a sense of abundance. Seeing overflowing fruit bowls and nuts in glass jars is a visual feast; the sight of it makes us feel contented. Kitchens where evidence of food is hidden lack warmth. Decorate with a necklace of garlic, a few jars of sprouting seeds, and pots of fragrant herbs.

On an environmental note: your kitchen is the processing plant at the end of a long, complicated food chain, and like any manufacturing site, it produces waste. If you buy food in packages, opt for those made out of cardboard, cellophane, or paper, which are biodegradable.

Play an active part in looking after the environment: take advantage of local recycling schemes; choose glass bottles over plastic; and where possible, turn vegetable material into compost for the garden.

top right: **Fresh vegetables await the chop. Nothing minces herbs finer than a specially designed antique herb-cutting knife.**

bottom right: **For full, potent flavours, season food wth fresh, rich herbs and spices.**

vital ingredients

Whether humble or gourmet, our food originates from land and sea. As Italian food ambassador Antonio Carluccio states in *Carluccio's Complete Italian Food*, rustic or real food comes straight from its source. It is 'about ripe fruit picked off the tree and eaten while still warm from the sun, fish straight from the water, meat reared and butchered with skill, wine made with the genuine local grapes and matured in ancient barrels, organic vegetables just dug from richly manured fields with the earth still clinging to their roots.' The idyll seems so far removed from our urban world that it seems like a vague, forgotten dream. Yet, as he states: 'This isn't just a romantic notion – this is how food should be!'

In the country, food is dependent on the kindness of the seasons. Weather conditions, the right time for harvesting, and the available methods of drying, storing, bottling, and preserving tend to determine what ends up on the table.

Supermarkets have divorced us from nature's seasonal selection and severed us from its manufacturing process. Instead, large outlets propagate us towards prewashed, preprepared, prepackaged vegetables, meats, and fruits, advising us to adhere to sell-by and best-by labels rather than depend on our nostrils to appraise whether food is ripe or not. Our edibles are so mass-manufactured, ready-made, boned, and filleted that we no longer register where it comes from. We wince when we see a fish's head and squirm when we find an insect crawling on a lettuce leaf.

We can no longer afford to be benignly oblivious to our food sources. The spectre of genetically modified foods, BSE (Mad Cow's Disease), chemically dependent farming, and endless health scares of recent years have demonstrated that we can't rest on the laurels of mass-produced foodstuffs. As a reaction, the demand for organic produce has burgeoned. Awakened to the difference in taste between a real tomato and its insipid, mass-farmed counterpart, our consumerism has finally extended beyond two-for-one specials, and wide aisles, back to its real source: the countryside.

Country has taken on a new meaning. Hard-core urbanites are hiring out-of-town allotments to grow their own fruit and vegetables, herb-strewn window boxes are gracing city ledges instead of geraniums, and local specialist shops – once shunned for the convenience of supermarkets – are regaining long-lost patrons.

Never missing out on a new source of revenue, supermarkets, responding to consumer demands, are now championing organic food. The adage 'You are what you eat' has become 'You are what you buy' and for once consumers are voting with their wallets.

For rosy-cheeked good health, ensure the food you consume is always absolutely fresh. If you don't buy organic vegetables, make sure they are well prepared; peel and wash, removing all chemical residues. To maintain vitamins, trace elements, minerals, and fibre, eat fruit and vegetables raw or barely cooked.

top left: **Golden olive oil. Good for the skin; good for the heart.**

bottom left: **Ingredients in this faux-peasant dish, such as parma ham, chicken, sun-dried tomatoes, and basil, have been used since the beginning of rustic *l'art culinaire*.**

top right: **Top of the rustic dining experience with smooth glass, antique cutlery, and chunky plates.**

bottom right: **Nothing beats the flavour and aroma of freshly baked organic bread.**

Enjoy preparing food, savouring colour, texture and aroma – the simplest inspirations behind a meal – and keep recipes uncomplicated, allowing freshness and flavour to take the limelight. Add herbs for interest, and season only with ground peppercorns and fresh sea salt.

Make your own herb teas (see page 82 for Moroccan tea), drinks (see pages 122–123 for details), and bake your own breads from organic flour.

Whenever you can, buy from producers direct and cultivate a relationship with them, or utilize the services of a number of organic companies who deliver direct from farm to door.

And try growing your own. Kitchen windowsills are excellent mini-glass houses for growing herbs and sprouts. Basil, lavender, rosemary, chervil, and parsley will flourish with a little love – and water. Mung beans and nutty tasting alfalfa (lucerne) sprouts are healthy additions to salads; to grow, place in glass jars under a cheese cloth and rinse the seeds twice daily with mineral water.

Most herbs are mobile movers. Marjoram, mint, sage, thyme, parsley, peppermint, fennel, dill, camomile, chervil, rocket, and others can be moved indoors or out depending on the season. Sun lovers such as basil and coriander are delicate, so keep them sill-bound. And if you are feeling a little more enthusiastic, turn a small patch of your backyard over into a kitchen garden, and grow your own salad greens and vegetables.

ginger beer

Originally drunk by peasants as a thirst-quencher at harvest time, ginger beer is a wonderfully refreshing beverage. Make it in large batches to last the whole summer long.

1 Put the yeast into a glass jar or bowl big enough to hold at least a pint. Pour in the water, and add a level tablespoon each of ginger and sugar. Cover the bowl with a clean linen cloth.

2 The next day feed the 'bug' with a heaped teaspoon each of ginger and sugar and cover again with the cloth.

3 About ten days later separate the sediment from the base liquid by straining it through a muslin-lined sieve into another bowl. (If you want to make further batches of beer, divide the sediment into two more glass jars, topping them up with water, ginger, and sugar.) To transform your base liquid into beer, dissolve the sugar into the boiling water and add the juice of the warmed lemons. Add the cold water to the bucket and stir well. Stir in the base liquid and top up with cold water until you have filled the bucket, blending the whole mixture together.

4 Pour the mixture into the bottles, and leave to stand for a few hours before corking. Add a few raisins, then cork. Sometimes, ginger beer might turn out to be more lively than you anticipate, so don't ram the corks down too hard otherwise the bottle may burst – it's better that the cork just pops out. Leave the bottles in a dark cupboard at room temperature for about two weeks. When the beer is ready, the raisins will rise to the top. Before opening, chill thoroughly.

YOU WILL NEED:
For 8 litres/16 pints of ginger beer

* 50g/2oz baker's yeast
* Glass jars or bowls
* 0.5 litres/1 pint water
* 1 level tbsp ground ginger
* 1 level tbsp granulated sugar
* Clean cloth or linen
* Wooden spoon
* 1 tsp ground ginger
* 1 tsp granulated sugar
* Muslin-lined sieve
* 1kg/2lb granulated sugar
* 1 litre/2 pints boiling water
* Juice of 6–8 lemons, warmed
* 9-litre/2-gallon bucket, sterilized
* 4.5 litres/1 gallon cold water
* Raisins
* Selection vintage ginger beer or lemonade bottles
* Plastic funnel
* Sterilized corks

relaxing

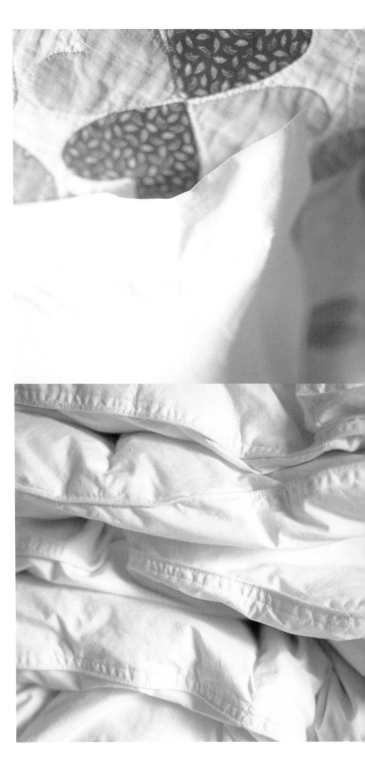

bed as a nest

Our beds are like nests. We line them with feathers, fabrics, and fur. We say we rise with the larks, or we are night owls. On a less atavistic level, bedrooms are our sanctuaries; our own private spaces where we close the door on the world, fleeing to the land of dreams.

At the hub of the bedroom is the bed. Aside from spending a third of our lives in these sleeping spaces, beds also bear witness to the cataclysmic events of our lives. We make love and conceive in a bed; we are born in a bed, and some of us die bed-ridden.

Experts suggest we should change our boudoir's mainstay once every ten years: poor sleep is linked to worn-out beds and backache. When purchasing a new bed, put it through its paces. Try lying on a showroom bed with minimal clothes on and alternating between positions (we toss and turn up to 70 times a night). A bed should fully support the spine while allowing the hips and shoulders to lie comfortably in their natural arc. When horizontally flat, the spine should form a shallow 'S' shape. Attempt this test: when you lie on a mattress slip your hand under the small of your back. If the hollow is devoid of mattress, it's too hard; if it's full then it's too spongy.

A supportive mattress and a solid base combine to make the best bed partners. Don't

left: A rustic retreat.

top right: Patchwork fields; patchwork quilts.

bottom right: Sink into a feather-filled duvet for a satisfying night's rest.

kid yourself into thinking a new mattress on an old base is the remedy for back pain: the two go hand in hand.

Once peasant mattresses were stuffed with hay, which is where the expression 'hitting the hay' has its origins. Traditional mattresses (still available) are peerless, consisting of a base of springs (more springs equals more support) sandwiched between layers of nature fibre padding such as coir, horsehair, or wool. A futon mattress, stuffed with cotton or wool, is another natural alternative, but often becomes lumpy if not properly cared for with regular turning and shaking. Turn and air all mattresses at least twice yearly.

When it comes to keeping warm, duvets are indispensable. Opt for a model with a box construction, where the filling (preferably natural, preferably down) is evenly distributed within individual compartments to prevent the feathers from gathering at one end. Always buy the size bigger than you need to provide ample no-need-to-fight-for-it coverage.

For sheets, nothing but natural fibres will do. Linen is simply the best. For a luxurious duvet cover try sewing together two linen sheets, with a zipper at one end, then stuffing it with a 100 per cent goose down duvet.

The most soporific bedrooms are dark, well aired and quiet, but it's surprising how many aren't. To minimize noise, the ancient art of feng shui (often rooted in practicality) advocates placing the room as far as possible from the main entrance of the house and the nearest road. If that's impossible, then consider soundproofing and double-glazing. For pleasant dreams, feng shui also recommends aligning your bed along a north-south axis, in harmony with the earth's magnetic field. To wake up with a clear head, always sleep with the window slightly open.

a lavender pillow

To sleep the sleep of kings, make a lavender-filled bag and tuck it between the pillow and its case. Lavender is reputed to have relaxing qualities, alleviating symptoms of stress and curing insomnia.

Make a herb sachet with dried lavender (dry by hanging the stems upside down in a dark cupboard) and fill up a small, flatly shaped cotton bag. To intensify the scent, add a few drops of essential lavender oil or a drop or two of rosemary and oregano oils.

relaxing 127

the living room

Never formal, austere, or pretentious, a rustic living room is one in which you can simply live. Whether relaxing alone in a favourite chair, or on a voluminous sofa with loved ones, choose furniture that is easy and informal. Rather than going for the classic three-piece suite, build up an interior with an assortment of chairs and a sofa, reupholstering them in identical or complementary fabrics, or painting them in the same shade of paint to achieve a visual cohesion. Arrange the layout so that the fireplace or hearth is the focal point of the living room, not the attention-grabbing television.

Living rooms are sun worshippers, so make sure yours basks in its rays. To invite light indoors or create views to the outside world, extend window frames, punch out skylights, and install French doors. In the northern hemisphere, living rooms are most effective at catching the sun's rays when positioned 30 degrees off true South. Otherwise ensure artificial light is ambient and atmospheric.

In the winter, make the living room deliciously cozy, but don't bake. Insulate with thick, woollen curtains, and use draught excluders to stop draughts snaking up under doors. Play furnishing dress-ups, revamping your sofas and armchairs with tactile warm-coloured coverings. For curling up with a good book, consider creating a fur-lined cushion-stuffed sleeping nook. Don't forget to let the cold air blast through occasionally, replacing stale air with fresh.

In the spring, it's all change. Ensure windows are gleaming, and deport heavy soft furnishings to cupboards, replacing them with cool-hued light, airy, chair covers and soft flimsy curtains. Try relocating the sofa from the fireside to underneath a window.

left: **Make the living room bright and inviting. In this lounge, light floods in from a large window, and from the level above.**

right: **An old chaise longue is given a new lease of life reclothed in modern fabric.**

outdoor living

Summer is about pure rustic living. Decamp the entire living room to the garden. It's hardly a new concept – outdoor living and dining al fresco are an intrinsic part of Mediterranean life. You'll discover casual lounge furniture masquerades as its outdoor equivalent. Wicker basket chairs, wooden benches, rattan sofas, cotton throws and beanbags have a secret double life waiting to be let off the leash.

Just as sofas and furnishings naturally blend with an interior, so should outdoor furniture be hewn from natural materials, harmonizing with the exterior. Ban plastic bucket seats and tables. Instead, strew about oversized cushions and woollen rugs, or for total relaxation, sew together a hammock and string it between two steadfast trees (see pages 134–135 for details), then recline in the shade, sipping an ice-cold glass of fresh ginger beer.

left: **Perchance to dream. The perfect place for an outdoor siesta.**

right: **Indoor furniture takes a hike outdoors and looks equally at home.**

Merge the area between indoors and out by creating a deck, patio, or pergola in the immediate area outside your French windows. Allow climbers such as honeysuckle, ivy, and climbing roses to take hold and provide a little cooling shade. Introduce a few garden tubs and hanging baskets overflowing with a variety of summer flowers.

Venturing further outside with your 'outdoor room', choose a sheltered position under trees, or a fenced-off area nearer to the house, to prevent your paper napkins from turning into impromptu kites. Near the places where you're likely to sit and sup, try planting herbs and scented plants, particularly honeysuckle, which releases its fragrant perfume into the night.

Think *A Midsummer Night's Dream*. Come nightfall, your garden should come to life with mystery and mood. Common techniques include silhouetting, spotlighting and uplighting, but try more off-beat techniques such as moonlighting (place lights in a tree to case a soft downward light); 'grazing' (highlight a textured surface such as a rock wall); or mirror lighting (where light is reflected off water or glass surfaces).

Hide lights behind plants, back lighting sculptural shapes and colours. Illuminate a garden statue, or sprinkle leaves on an uplighter to create dappled light, nature's version of stained glass. Think optical illusion: place spotlights around the perimeter or cast light over a wall with a concealed spotlight to add depth and a delusion of grandeur. Keep lighting flexible with spiked garden light fittings or

directional spotlights to change as your garden evolves. On a practical note, before you start haphazardly erecting a system, think safety first: consult a qualified electrician and construct a plan.

Candles, flares, and storm lanterns are the most beautiful ways of inviting ambient light into your garden. Become like diva agent Peggy Ramsay (as reported in Simon Callow's *Love is Where it Falls*): 'She steered us into the garden …a vision in itself. With a hundred candles in small jars placed across the flowerbed, she had transformed what I took to be a small non-descript space into a shimmering grotto'. Simply divine, simply rustic.

left: A rustic version of a high-backed Mackintosh chair. Collect a dozen for a formal outdoor dinner.

right: Hang sturdy lanterns in the garden at night for a soft light.

hammock

On a sunny afternoon, there's nothing more relaxing than swinging in a hammock, book in hand, under a shady tree.

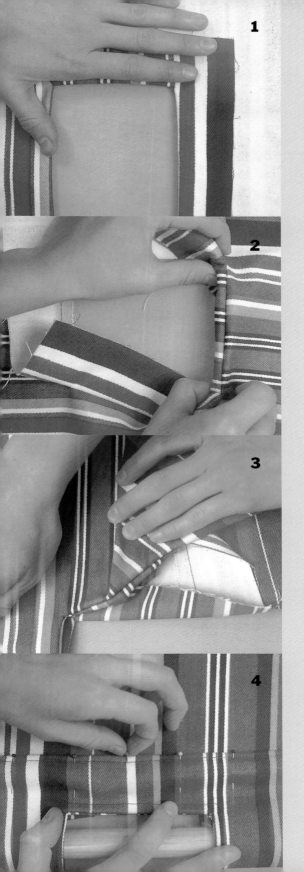

1 From your canvas, cut a piece 250cm/100in long for the hammock. If your fabric is not 120cm/48in in width, you will need to hem the raw sides, by adding a seam allowance of 3cm/1¼in, and turning the material over twice before sewing. From the remaining canvas, cut ten pieces each measuring 20 x 20cm/8 x 8in. For each end of the hammock, divide the fabric up into six equal parts and mark with pins approximately 10cm/4in from the edge. Take five fabric squares and centre one over each pin mark. Pin right sides together. In a line approximately 5cm/2in from the perimeter edge of each fabric square, stitch the two pieces together. Cut out the inner section (cutting through both layers of fabric), and snip into the corners.

2 Press the seam open, then push the fabric flap through to the reverse of the hammock and machine sew 1cm/ ½ in in from the seam.

3 With the hammock face down, turn over each end first 2.5cm/1in, then 10cm/4in and smooth out the loops.

4 Pin and machine stitch in place. With the drill, make a hole (large enough for the rope to pass through), approximately 2.5cm/1in from the ends of each length of dowelling. Thread the dowelling through the loops at each end of the hammock. Take each length of rope, thread on a curtain ring, and pass the end through the holes in each dowelling rod and secure with a tight knot. To hang the hammock, pass another length of rope through each curtain ring and tie between two suitably strong trees.

YOU WILL NEED:
* 300 x 120cm/120 x 48in wide strong stripy canvas
* Two lengths of 130cm/52in dowelling, 2.5cm/1in in diameter
* 250cm/100in strong thick rope or sash cord, cut in half
* 2 large curtain rings
* Sewing machine
* Sewing kit
* Electric drill and drill bits
* Iron

putting the
look together

creating the modern rustic look is an organic process that takes time – and commitment. Some decorative touches – the perfect shade of paint for a natural whitewash, the just-so sofa, the right curtain fabric – may take some effort tracking down, but the end result is a timeless, classic look that will be well worth that little extra effort. And of course, even then the modern rustic home is never really 'finished': as in nature, it's mutable, constantly changing with the ebb and flow of the seasons.

The 'interior recipe' for modern rustic must start with the architecture. Take two backdrops, the floors and the walls. Strip back the skin to reveal the rustic bones, such as old wood flooring, or raw plaster walls. Otherwise, cover them with naturally derived products (wood, cork, tiles, organic paint), all materials that allow the surfaces underneath to breathe.

Think about the country's biggest drawcards – natural light, air and views, and create connections to the outside world through windows and doors. Consider their style and shape, and keep window dressings simple. Salvage old wooden doors, and add antique door handles and knockers.

Against these backdrops, arrange furniture and furnishings, balancing modern backdrops with antique furniture, and old settings with organic, contemporary items. Then add your soft furnishings. To fit in with the modern rustic blend, the fabric fibres and dyes that make up your cushions, squabs, curtains, and bed linen should be derived from natural sources, such as plants (linen, hessian, and cotton), and animals (silk and wool). Play with the space you have, contrasting grand hulking sofas with small areas of detail, such as a cluster of beach stones or a sculpture of driftwood fragments. Finally add dabs of colour which come directly from, or mimic, nature's own palette in accessories such as vases, displays, throws, or ornaments.

Visual images help as a reference point. It's often difficult to imprint the overall feel in your mind's eye, or remember the exact nuances of your existing space when you're out hunting for materials and furniture. Try an interior designer's trick and create a storyboard or a mini flick book.

left: Create your own arcadia. Blend old and new, rough and smooth, modern and rustic.

Both work in much the same way. A carry-around flick book is like your personal shopping assistant – it will keep you on track. To create one, buy a small, plain exercise book, take photos of your current interior (also noting its measurements), then source inspirational images from newspapers, product brochures, magazines, catalogues, and postcards, and paste these alongside the shots of your rooms. Some of these can be 'wish' pictures; and it's surprising how often once you have a particular thing in mind something similar turns up.

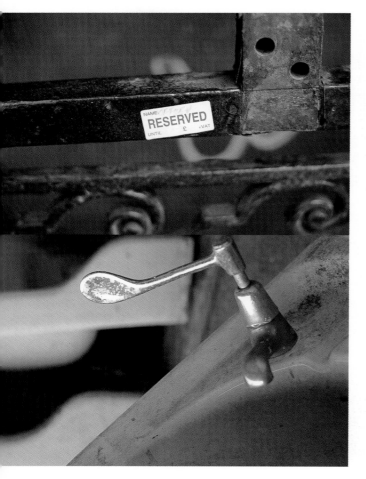

Before you purchase anything, glance through the flick book to discern whether your chosen product marries with the modern rustic ethos, your existing possessions, and the emerging colour scheme. Prior to selecting fabric and paints, collate swatches and stick them side-by-side. Utilize the book further by taking and pasting in Polaroid snaps of potential buys (particularly useful for larger purchases such as sofas and beds). Armed with images of possible fabrics, paints, and furniture, you can weigh up whether objects, textures, and materials will harmonize.

A storyboard is essentially the same idea though obviously not as portable as a flick book. Take a large sheet of cardboard, then pin up a layout of the room you want to decorate and add different visuals (swatches, Polaroids, paint charts, etc.) onto the board, then consider how the whole look will come to life.

Don't forget nature itself, modern rustic's real inspiration. While you're planning the overall scheme, simply take a day out and go walking through the forest, or strolling along the beach, observing the dance of colours, shapes, scents, and sounds. Then on your return, look at your home with a fresh eye and, thinking of nature, try answering a check list from Kahlil Gibran's *The Prophet*:

'Have you peace, the quiet urge that reveals your power?
Have you remembrances, the glimmering arches that span the summits of the mind?
Have you beauty, that leads the heart from things fashioned of wood and stone to
    the holy mountain?
Tell me, have you these things in your houses?'

left: Find lost treasures and put your name on them. In old salvage yards, it's a case of see it, like it, buy it, so go armed with cash, courage, and vision.

right: Things that inspire: clippings, Polaroids, leaves and the great, great outdoors.

Paint

Frescoes
Crumbling paint
Rag n' roll
Gold leaf

ark leath
terracotta
rust
green
Olive green

credits

All photography credited to Chris Tubbs apart from the following:

Livingetc Magazine: pp 26 (Ed Reeve); 128 (Peter Aprahamian).
MQ Publications Ltd: pp 42 top, 48 bottom, 53 bottom, 62, 63 bottom (Polly Wreford); p. 56 top (Lucinda Symons); pp 65, 75 (Claude Simon); pp 67, 130 right (Olivier Maynard).

We would like to extend our warm thanks to the following people:

Ljiljana Baird, for giving us this wonderful opportunity; Alison Moss for her patience and guidance; Amanda Smith for her ingenious projects; and the team at ELLE DECO for their inspiration. We are indebted to the people who have thrown open their doors to us, particularly Andrea McGarvie-Munn, who introduced us to the beautiful homes of her friends, Madame Gabrielle Gastinel, feted potter Gerard Lachens, Sama; Juliette Dearden, Peter Lowe, and Zaro Weil. Special thanks to Jane Stalker (handmade soap project), Lauren (dish on page 120), Mike Paul, Dame and Murray H, Dominique, Dizzy and Brian Ward. *Ali Hanan and Chris Tubbs*

Useful Addresses

Jacques Brest Ceramiques
(Handmade tile factory in the south of France)
Quartier des Arnauds,
83690 Salernes, France
(00 33 494706065)
(See photos p. 38)

Gerard Lachens *(Potter)*
(00 33 492746611)

Blustin-Heath Design *(Architects)*
First Floor, 14 Bacon Street,
London E1 6LF
(0207 739 9618)
(see photo p. 4)

Robert Young Antiques
(Antique dealer)
68 Battersea Road,
London SW11 3AG
(0207 228 7847)
(See photos pp 88, 89 bottom, 94)

Josephine Ryan
(Antiques and interior design)
63 Abbeville Road,
London SW4 9JW
(0208 675 3900)
(See photos pp 41, 50, 56 bottom, 83, 115 top, 136)

Stephen Collier
(Contemporary florist)
(0208 968 8952)
(See photos p. 95 top and bottom)

Andrea McGarvie-Munn
Mas des Garviers,
Pourrieres, France
(00 33 494784038)
(See photos pp 37, 60)
Call for details of her rustic retreat

Babington House *(Rural sanctuary)*
Kilmersdon,
Frome,
Somerset BA11 3RW
(01373 812266)
(See photos pp 102, 124)
Call for details

Lucy Williams *(Furniture designer)*
(01892 724375)
(See photos pp 49, 132)

Christina Wilson *(Interior designer)*
(0207 380 1298)
(See photos pp 15, 101, 114)

Angela D'Court Design
(0208 340 6135)
(See photos pp 51, 54, 55)

Freire Wright
(0207 625 5823)

project index

painted chair
pages 30-31

patchwork cushions
pages 44-45

rugged stool
pages 58-59

tin lanterns
pages 68-69

fur throw
pages 78-79

scented candles
pages 86- 87

nature paper prints
pages 96-97

handmade soap
pages 110-111

ginger beer
pages 122-123

hammock
pages 134-135

index

Numbers in *italics* indicate captions.

air, fresh 85, *109*, 137
antique shops 16, 91
armchairs 47, *53*, 70
aromatherapy 84, *85*, 107, 109

bamboo 47
barn, converted *13*, *53*
baskets *13*, 54, 56, *56*
bathing 100-111
bathrooms 26, 36, 62, 94
    design 104-6
beams 14, 70, *107*
beanbags 130
bed linen *40*, *42*, 43, 76, *127*,
    137
bedrooms 26, 43, 125, 127
beds 125, 127, *127*
beeswax 27, 38
benches 130
blankets 43, *53*, 76
blinds 62, *63*, 106
bottles *16*, 95
brick *26*, 27, 33, 36, *36*, 39, 70
butcher's block 114, *114*

calico 43
candelabra *64*, 67
candles 67, *67*, 70, *70*, 95, 135
    scented 86-7
cane 47, 49
canvas 63

car boot sales 16, 49
carpets 14, 33, 36, 42-3
cashmere *40*
ceilings 27
central heating 74
chairs 129, *133*
    bent wood 9, 47, 53
    dining *48*
    leather 15, *47*
    painted 30-31
    reupholstering 53
    'Thonet' 9, 47
    wicker *53*, 130
    wooden *48*, 49, *49*, 53
chaise longues 53, *129*
charity auctions 49
charity shops 16
chests *53*, 54
chimneys 73
clay 27, 39
coffee grinders *91*
coir 36, 127
colour 20-31
    neutral 26-7
    the origins of 20
    the seasonal palette 20-26
    warm/cool 26
cork 27, 38, 106, 117, 137
cotton 17, 40, *40*, 43, 127, 130,
    137
couches 70
crochet *61*
crockery 91
cupboards 54, *54*, 56, 129

curtains 62, 63, *63*, 76, *76*, 129, 137
    door *61*
cushions 14, 43, *53*, 70, 129, 137
    patchwork 44-5

day beds 53
detail 88-97
dining rooms 26, 53, 115
distemper 20, 27, 28
doorknobs 89, *89*
doors, antique 137
dressing gown *40*
duvets 43, *125*, 127
dyes, natural 20, 40, 137

eating 112-23
emulsion 38
entrance halls 36
essential oils 84, *85*, 107, 109
estate sales 16, 49
exfoliation *100*, 109

fabrics 40-43
    antique *17*
    natural 14
feng shui 127
fireplaces 15, 70, *95*, 129
fires 70, 73, *74*
flagstones 33
flares 133
flea markets 16, *17*, 49, 91
flick books 137-8
floor coverings 33, 36
floorboards 15, *26*, 33

floors 14, 36, 39, 137
flowers *81*, 82, 83, 95, 133
food *116*, 117, 119-21
furniture
    plastic 47
    wooden 47

ginger beer 122-3
glasses *91*
granite 33, 116

hammock 130, 134-5
hatboxes 56, *56*
hearth 70, 73, 129
heat 70-79
hemp 43
herbs 82-3, 107, 121, 127, *127*, 133
hessian 43, 56, 137
horsehair 43, 127

insulation 76, 129
internet auction sites 16, 17
ironwork 14

Jacuzzis 106
jars *54*, 91, 114, *116*
junk shops 16, 91
jute 36

kettle *91*
kitchens 26, 36, 39, *39*, 112-21
knife rack *54*

lace *42*, 43, 56

First published in the United Kingdom in 2000 by Cassell & Co
Text copyright © Ali Hanan, 2000
Photographs © Chris Tubbs, 2000
Design and layout © MQ Publications Ltd, 2000

The publisher has endeavoured to ensure that all project instructions are accurate. However, due to variations in
readers' individual skill and materials available, the publisher cannot accept responsibility for damages or losses
resulting from the instructions herein. All instructions should be studied and clearly understood before beginning
any project.

Livingetc is published eleven times per year by IPC Magazines Limited, Kings Reach Tower, Stamford Street,
London SE1 9LS. For subscription enquiries and orders please call 01444 445555 (fax no: 01444 445599).
For credit card orders call the subscription credit card hotline (UK orders only) on 01622 778778.

A CIP catalogue record for this book is available from the British Library

ISBN 0-304-35435-X

Series Editor: Ljiljana Baird
Editor: Alison Moss
Projects: Amanda Smith
Designer: Bet Ayer

Cassell & Co, Wellington House, 125 Strand, London WC2R 0BB